FROM STAGE
TO SCREEN

FROM STAGE TO SCREEN

A Theatre Actor's Guide to Working on Camera

BILL BRITTEN

B L O O M S B U R Y

LONDON • NEW DELHI • NEW YORK • SYDNEY

Bloomsbury Methuen Drama

An imprint of Bloomsbury Publishing Plc

50 Bedford Square
London
WC1B 3DP
UK

1385 Broadway
New York
NY 10018
USA

www.bloomsbury.com

Bloomsbury is a registered trade mark of Bloomsbury Publishing Plc

First published 2015

Copyright © Bill Britten 2015

Image of Tommie Smith and John Carlos published with permission.
Copyright © PA Images
Extracts from *Body Heat* reproduced by permission of Warner Bros.
Copyright © 1981.

British Library Cataloguing-in-Publication Data
A catalogue record for this book is available from the British Library.

ISBN: PB: 978-1-4081-8546-9
ePDF: 978-1-4725-2264-1
ePub: 978-1-4081-8490-5

Library of Congress Cataloging-in-Publication Data
Britten, Bill.
From stage to screen : a theater actor's guide to working on camera/Bill Britten.
pages cm
Summary: "From Stage to Screen is a handbook for the professional actor
packed with advice on how to make the transition and fully prepare for
a TV or film role"– Provided by publisher.
ISBN 978-1-4081-8546-9 (paperback)
1. Acting. I. Title.
PN2061.B75 2015
792.02'8–dc23
2014009098

Typeset by Deanta Global Publishing Services, Chennai, India
Printed and bound in India

CONTENTS

ACKNOWLEDGEMENTS

With grateful thanks to:

Hugh Bonneville
Adrian Lester
Sir Ben Kingsley
Juliet Stevenson
Helen Tulley
Sally Holloway
Garry Hayden
Jon Pascoe
Eleanor Fusaro
Deepal Parmar
Madam J. H. Lee
Scott Cleverdon
Assumpta Serna
Michael Maynard

FOREWORD

One of my first TV jobs – I had two lines. I spotted the star on the dining bus and nervously asked if it would be all right to run the dialogue before going on set to rehearse. I can still see the expression on his face: a mixture of surprise, irritation and perhaps a soupçon of pity. With a deep sigh he reluctantly blah-blah'd through the brief scene with me. I felt about an inch high. Maybe I had made some filming faux pas about disturbing actors in their down time; I didn't know the rules. Or maybe he was just being a jerk. Either way, I felt totally out of my depth in this strange environment, hanging around in isolation while the crew got on with driving the production – the complete opposite to life in the theatre, which was the life I knew.

As a kid I was told that screen acting was the preserve of the Americans, whereas British actors owned the stage. A ridiculous generalization but hey, I was 10 and my drama teacher said it was so. Throughout my teens this skewed misconception became even more twisted and I began to suspect that screen and stage were such different disciplines that they might as well be two languages, each foreign to the other.

Well, having now spent the first dozen years of my working life in the theatre and the second largely in front of a camera, I've learnt that of course nationality doesn't come into it and that the two worlds are not in fact galaxies apart. They may have different vocabularies but ultimately they speak the same tongue, communicating ideas through the entertaining business.

Once upon a time I auditioned three times for a movie, for smaller and smaller roles. As the director told me, this was a low budget film that was to be shot on an incredibly tight schedule. He needed actors who understood working on camera, who knew how to hit their marks;

there would be no time for basic errors. I had no film or TV experience to speak of, so I wasn't cast. At least, that's what they said to my agent, which gave me a brilliant excuse to go to the pub and whinge for a few hours. It also made me determined to get in front of a camera as soon as possible so that the accusation of lacking technical know-how couldn't be levelled at me again. Next time they'd just have to think up another reason for not casting me. Next time maybe they'd just have to tell me I was rubbish. The movie in question was *Four Weddings and a Funeral*. It did OK.

I began to seek out guides to acting on screen. Some were filled with psychobabble, others with squiggly diagrams. None spoke to me, a theatre practitioner who knew a bit about film but not much. Well aware that a little knowledge is a dangerous thing I wanted to learn more about not just the theory but the practicalities of being an actor on a film set – the area of our industry in which, perhaps more than any other, time is money and explanation a luxury. I wanted to feel better prepared for the day when someone finally gave me a break.

I could have done with a book like this one.

Hugh Bonneville

INTRODUCTION

Most of us come to acting through the stage. From school drama classes and reading out loud in lessons, we progress to performing in assemblies and plays. At home we may be encouraged by parents and friends to put on little playlets. As we become more socially skilled, we get better at telling jokes and stories to our friends to make them laugh or sympathize with us.

There's one consistent element in all this: a live audience. We learn, little by little, to sense people's reaction and to adapt what we do in response. When it comes to working on screen, many experienced stage actors are lost because this feedback loop simply doesn't exist and because the working conditions of filming are so very different to the theatre.

So this book is intended to help those who have some experience on stage and would like to develop their ability on screen, but don't want to experiment on the job!

It's aimed at three imaginary readers:

1   the beginner–professional – the working professional, probably trained as a stage actor, who wants to work (more) on screen and is aware that his previous experience and training don't really equip him to handle screen work comfortably

2   the student, training to become a professional actor or studying drama with an ambition to act professionally

3   those with an interest in professional acting, perhaps considering training and wondering which of the bewildering array of courses to apply to.

I worked professionally as an actor on stage and screen for 10 years, towards the end of which I began to direct, spending the next 15 years directing film and television drama. So what I shall say is based partly on my experience of what it's like to act in the two media and partly on my observations as a director. In particular, in many, many months spent poring over actors' performances in cutting rooms, I began to notice things about what *works* on screen. So I shall come at it from both angles: the actor's and the director/audience's experience.

One of the choices any author has to make is whether to refer to '*he or she*' throughout (laborious), alternate the genders (confusing) or just use one throughout. I'm going for the third option so '*he*' refers to any actor.

And finally, an apology to any film editors who might read this book if I appear to attribute all the editing decisions to the director. I'm well aware that much of the work in post-production is done by the editor, but to keep making reference to this throughout the book would rapidly become tiresome and, let's face it, actors are primarily interested in pleasing the job-giving director.

1
LET'S PRETEND

Acting is about inhabiting a fictional reality. There are many internal
barriers we must overcome in order to access free acting. The
analytical thinking that our education system trains in us can be one
of these barriers, but we can retrain ourselves to be spontaneous
and impulsive without becoming impossible to work with.

Acting is easy

'*Let's pretend is the original impulse of acting*' – Laurence Olivier.

Acting is child's play. Literally. Throughout history, children the world
over have always played *let's pretend*. The poorest child on earth will
pick up a bunch of rags, pretend it's a doll and talk to it. Put several
children together and they will quickly invent some game that involves
make-believe.

Of course play is not just fooling around. It's the means by which we
practise the skills we need to navigate the world and imaginative play
is no different. Adults tend to regard play as simply a diversion, a bit of
indulgent fun to be enjoyed in our leisure time once the serious business
of work is over. Yet, pretending is a fundamental way of understanding
the world and of practising behaviour. What's more, it's something we
never truly leave behind. We rehearse conversations in our heads,
running through what we will say and coming up with pithy retorts to

the responses we imagine will come our way. The conversation rarely actually goes the way we anticipated, but the practice helps us prepare nonetheless.

The Greeks had a word 'mimesis' that describes this innate human capacity to explore imagined or alternate realities. As we start to explore what acting is, perhaps it's useful to consider three levels of mimesis.

The first is imagination without boundaries. Anything can be anything, anyone can be anyone. These are the wondrous children's games where one child is Harry Potter, another is Buzz Lightyear, the carpet is the sea and the sofa is a camel. No resemblance to reality is needed and imagination has no limits. Like many parents, I used to find these games with my children depressingly difficult to play. Something inside me gets bogged down with reality and I want to point out that if you're Harry Potter, I can't be Buzz Lightyear because he comes from a different film and, anyway, camels can't swim. But these technicalities don't bother 3-year-olds. (And as it turns out, camels can swim. I just checked. 2-0 to the kids.)

As we get older and start to recognize patterns in the world and exercise our ability to influence things, we start to impose structure on our games, agreeing on boundaries so that the game *works*. Arguments break out if a player does something that contradicts the game's internal logic.

This internal logic takes us into the second level of mimesis where the pretence is about specific scenarios. Before we can play *let's-pretend*, we need to agree on the boundaries and the rules. At the heart of this is a collusion between the actors about the dramatic scenario. We agree who's who and what the situation is and then play it out.

The third level of mimesis involves not only a specific dramatic scenario, but a script with predetermined dialogue and actions as well as outcomes. This is the territory of the professional and it's what we'll explore in relation to the screen.

At first sight, the task of truthfully and spontaneously inhabiting something that's been concocted by a writer can seem bewilderingly contradictory. But, in fact, it is also remarkably simple. You and the other actors agree on the fictional world and who you are within it. Then you play the same game of *let's-pretend* but with certain things you have to say and do. And that's it.

What the writer does, first and foremost, is construct the story through its architecture. A central character pursues something he desires, and narrative events – be they physical actions or words spoken – move the story forward to a resolution.

But no matter how many car crashes or explosions take place, what the audience engages with emotionally is the experience of the characters as they journey through this structure. And no matter how intricate the dialogue or detailed the directions, the author can only scratch the surface of truly defining the character's inner world; such is the richness and complexity of the human experience. So while a good writer will plot an emotional journey through a scene, and while some of this may be hinted at by the dialogue, most of it is not. Most of it, in fact, goes on between the lines. And it's the actor who writes that script.

Judi Dench: '*Acting is not what you say, it's what you don't say.*'

We probably all know from seeing more than one production of the same play, if you put the same words in the mouths of two different actors, you will see two wholly different human beings with two different journeys through the same story. And this brings us to a central fact about acting: there is no right way of playing a scene. There are wrong ways certainly – ways that don't ring true or don't give sufficient weight to what the story needs. But there are many, many pathways through every story and every scene that do the job in terms of narrative development and simultaneously create a unique, credible human character with a rich inner world.

Recognizing that you, the performer, get to make most of the choices about this inner world can be intensely liberating. What's more, it applies just as much to the smaller parts as to the lead. '*There are no such things as small parts, only small actors.*' All right, let's be honest, there are parts so small that we're frankly not interested in the character's inner world – the spear-carrier or the policeman who brings in the suspect for questioning perhaps. But even with these parts we recognize the difference between a spear-carrier or copper who's engaged in the world of the story and a bored actor who's going through the motions to fulfil a function. Indeed, it's amazing how one's eye is drawn to the extra in the background who's either overacting or bored because it's the fourteenth take. We want the smaller parts to be rich and detailed as human beings.

The professional actor brings third-level mimesis to the specific words and actions of the script, responding spontaneously and organically to what goes on around him. In so doing he creates a rich internal world and truthful emotional interaction – the communion that Stanislavski wrote about. And through watching this communion, the audience understands, on a deep level, how the character's emotions have been influenced and *why* he has said and done what the script dictates.

If you have done your preparation; *if* you have truly understood your character and his situation; *if* you have succeeded in turning a bunch of words on a page into a deep identification and embodiment of a human being; *if* you can really listen; *if* you can absolutely give yourself up to the fictional scenario, as a child does, then acting is easy. You can begin to work on an intuitive level, engaging wholly with the context and the characters, just behaving and reacting without thinking, similar to the way top sportspeople describe how they play when they're at their very best, *'in the zone'*, seeing the ball earlier, playing it effortlessly, making the right decisions without conscious thought.

The best acting is incredibly simple. Hugh Bonneville: '*Both disciplines – stage and screen – require you to listen, look people in the eye and tell the truth.*'

Acting is difficult

It won't have escaped your notice that the previous paragraph contains a lot of *'if'*s. To reach that state of simplicity – of openness and spontaneity and technical mastery – requires huge amounts of hard work and commitment, rigorous training and dedication. And, of course, a lot of talent. Because let's not pretend there aren't a handful of supremely gifted individuals who somehow seem to be able to do the above without the tiresome business of hard work and preparation. Those actors who just seem to start from somewhere different, with an engagement and a commitment and a lack of inhibition from the very beginning, much as there are some kids who just have superior innate coordination and a better eye for the ball. Lucky them.

But before we all disappear into a quagmire of envy, consider a couple of things. First, these actors have to master the technical requirements of the medium – stage or screen or radio – just like every other actor. And second, if they do not work to maintain their talent, to protect and nurture this balance between focus and freedom, they will not have a career. The world of show business has an endless appetite for novelty. It moves on and there are plenty of starlets who never progress beyond an initial burst of promise and attention, who occasionally pop up in some bit of telly and you think, *'I remember him. He was everywhere and then he just disappeared. I wonder where he's been for the last ten years?'* Sometimes the answer is 'drinking'. But more often, they were just lazy. They didn't put in the graft required to turn talent into expertise. They took their success for granted and complacency destroyed their careers. In short, they lacked professionalism.

(Of course, sometimes they were neither self-destructive nor lazy and were just plain unlucky but, hey, perhaps that compensates for their good fortune in possessing natural talent in the first place.)

Back to reality and the rest of us and this nirvana of free acting. My assumption is that if you are reading this book, either you are trained, are training or are considering training as an actor. One of the major jobs of drama schools and actor training, generally, is to help actors reconnect with this inner child who can give himself freely to *'let's pretend'*. And for most of us it is a question of *reconnection* because there's a lot of stuff that gets in the way. Lots of inhibitions and blocks and internal rules about behaviour that we need to let go of. To achieve this we have to cultivate a way of being, a way of engaging with the world and other people that gives us access to the impulses and feelings that will charge our acting with truth.

The trouble is, this way of being can often seem antisocial or childish or downright selfish. Certainly, sticking inflexibly to decorum and propriety and conventional behaviour isn't going to help us access the freedom we need. Lots of actors like to see themselves as unconventional and unorthodox and bohemian. But we also have friends and families and lovers. When we work, we have to collaborate and compromise and get along with people. We obey the social mores and conventions (or at least most of them) that enable us to function in society. So while we aim to be free and totally spontaneous in our work, we also have to manage our impulses so that we can live among our fellow human beings, and there's a bit of a contradiction there. But then contradictions abound in acting. Not least in that we're trying to be utterly spontaneous and truthful in conditions, both on stage and screen, which are hugely artificial. Well, suck it up because that's the job.

The intellectual actor

For many of those who aspire to be actors or to become better actors, the biggest challenge is to stop thinking and start feeling. Our education system trains young people in thinking and the prizes are given out for analytical skills. But fundamentally this is a cerebral engagement, impassive and rational. And this kind of education – especially at degree level – is often in direct opposition to what actors need to cultivate in themselves.

For much of our lives, we are served well by the ability to think logically about what's happening and make considered, rational decisions about what to do. Indeed, for most professions it's essential. I'm guessing we would all rather be operated on, or have our taxes done, by someone with the rigour of thinking to be able to analyse a situation and come up with a reliably intelligent plan of attack.

But the foremost job of an actor is to commit to the fictional world of a drama and this is not a cerebral activity. The qualities that will really make a performance – spontaneity, impulsiveness, emotional availability, unguarded vulnerability – are neither logical nor intellectual. And these are things we can deliberately cultivate in ourselves.

Nicolas Cage: *'I invite the entire spectrum, shall we call it, of feeling. Because that is my greatest resource as a film actor. I need to be able to feel everything, which is why I refuse to go on any kind of medication. Not that I need to! But my point is, I wouldn't even explore that, because it would get in the way of my instrument. Which is my emotional facility to be able to perform.'*

There may be a cost to this of course. Personally, I'm quite proud of my ability not to get railroaded by my immediate response. Only this morning my 12-year-old daughter did something that really annoyed me and I consciously had to stop myself responding in a petty and vengeful way by saying something unkind or depriving her of something. As I write this, I've completely forgotten what her offence was, which tells you something about its seriousness. But it illustrates the tension that exists between emotionality and impulsivity and the restraint and self-control that can make us better human beings. And the one will have an impact on the other.

There are lots of ways in which what I'm saying can be misunderstood, so let me clear up a few of them.

First, there's no romantic heroism to losing your temper and visiting your uninhibited emotions on those around you. There are plenty of actors for whom Heathcliff is the role model; actors who think it's OK – and kind of sexy – to indulge their emotions and rage and have tantrums, as if this is somehow justified by the work. Indeed, there are drama schools where it's seen as acceptable for everyone – students and tutors alike – to behave badly, on the grounds that it's inevitable, or even desirable freedom. I think this is nonsense. The job of the drama school is to help actors access their inner impulses and learn to manage them in productive ways. After all, an actor without control will be unable to participate in the collaboration that is filming. Not only will he have no friends but he won't be able deliver when the director calls *'action'*.

I'm not suggesting that great actors are not intelligent. In fact, I'd say it's impossible to be a great actor without being highly intelligent.

But it's not necessarily the kind of intelligence that earns you praise and qualifications at school.

But neither am I suggesting that the academically smart cannot be great actors. In the English-speaking world, there's too long a list of great actors with degrees from Oxbridge, Yale and Harvard for this to be plausible.

Actors certainly need the ability to analyse intellectually in order to understand the drama fully and make interesting choices. There's frequently a lot of analytical work that goes into researching and understanding the world of the drama and a lot of deduction required to piece together the clues in the script that go into creating a rich, thorough characterization.

But I **am** suggesting that there comes a point when actors, especially screen actors, must abandon the intellectual and commit themselves to the intuitive. And to some extent actors must cultivate in themselves a kind of anti-intellectualism that enables them just to **be**: to act and react spontaneously.

Developing yourself

There are profound inner qualities that you should aim to grow in yourself. You need to cultivate the ability to be uninhibited, to commit, to give yourself freely to the *now*. This is about so much more than a technical proficiency. It's about a whole approach to life.

Let me give you some examples of what I mean.

You're walking down the street and something catches your eye in a shop window or down a side turning. Ordinarily you might dismiss it and walk on by. Don't. Go and look. Practise following your impulses. Catch the moment of curiosity and get used to respecting it.

When you feel the impulse to do something but also feel embarrassed: do it anyway. Train yourself to take risks and get used to conquering the number one enemy of good acting: embarrassment. Alan Alda did a cartwheel as he walked to the stage in 1979 to collect a writing Emmy for M*A*S*H. What impresses me is the sheer audacity of doing it in front of all those people, with the attendant risks that: (a) it's not a very good cartwheel; and (b) people think you a fool for doing it. It's important to remember that taking risks means sometimes you will fail. Get used to looking at it this way: if you never fail, you're not taking enough risks.

> Sir Ken Robinson, noted educationalist: '*You will never do anything original, unless you are prepared to fail.*'

It's worth distinguishing between risk and recklessness. One has a reasonable chance of success and doesn't threaten ruin. The other has little chance of success and possibly has devastating consequences. Directors, on both stage and screen, should welcome risk. But few will welcome recklessness. The screen director's twin concerns are the quality of the work and meeting the schedule. Mess up his schedule and he won't hire you again.

But this shouldn't prevent you embracing the spirit of play. There is so much serious stuff to be dealt with as a grown-up. Quite apart from the necessity to run your life, pay the bills and so on, this seriousness has its place in your acting. But so do lightness and play and exploration. Keeping your sense of playfulness vibrant and agile takes dedication. And ironically, this is particularly true once you become a parent and have the real experts in play – children – around you.

When you feel yourself moved by something: don't fight it. Give into it and let yourself be moved. This is especially important for men because, certainly in the Western world, we are discouraged from a young age from being emotional. So for many of us it takes conscious effort to learn to accept our emotions and experience them in all their richness. For both sexes, much of adult emotional life is contained and constrained by ideas of appropriateness. We cauterize much of the complexity and depth in our emotional responses so as to protect ourselves from hurt and from the disapproval of others. So, my advice is to accept the hurt. Accept the disapproval. Live fully. Your emotions need to be available to you.

Emotional intelligence

Being open to your emotions is **not** the same as imposing them on other people in ways that are hurtful or damaging. *Experiencing* emotion does not preclude the possibility of *managing* emotion. It can, admittedly, be a difficult trick to pull off. There can appear to be a compelling argument that eliminating the blocks to truthful emotional response in your acting necessitates giving free rein to your truthful emotional response in life. But consider this: you're in a rehearsal or on set, between takes, and somebody – actor, technician, director, whoever – says something you don't like and your truthful emotional response is to want to thump them. What happens if we all allow our behaviour to be solely dictated by pure emotion, unmediated by awareness of others and oblivious of the consequences of our actions? Or perhaps the impulse is directed inwards – we are hurt and we want to cry or we are insulted and we want to walk off? What kind of chaos do we all end up working in if everyone simply follows their uninhibited emotions?

There is a difference between being emotional and emotionalizing – indulging emotions for their own sake. Emotional intelligence is not the denial of emotion, it's the intelligent management of emotion. Even the most hard core of Meisner-influenced *get-in-touch-with-your-emotions* teachers distinguish between what happens during the work and what happens outside the work.

This management of emotional access – making our emotions directly available to us as we work and yet still permitting us to function as responsible human beings – is one of the great challenges for an actor. While a few of the greats – Ian McKellen, Judi Dench, Denzel Washington – seem able to pull it off effortlessly, it's perhaps no surprise that some others are prone to bursting into tears whenever they receive an award or throwing tantrums when they don't get their own way. While I see nothing wrong with the former, the latter is no more acceptable here than anywhere else in life. It gets indulged when the culprit is a star who's worth a lot of money to the producers. But it doesn't have to be like this and it would be a mistake to think that bad behaviour is making them better actors. It just makes them a pain in the backside to be with.

The self-awareness and reflection that is involved in developing this kind of emotional intelligence is not for everyone and plenty of great actors don't do it consciously. But given that you're reading a book about how to improve your acting, perhaps it is something you're interested in cultivating. It certainly forms the core of my ambition for the actors I work with and underpins the approach I shall be taking here.

2
THE BIG DIFFERENCES

There are three primary differences between stage and screen:

1 The camera comes so close there is no need to project. The screen actor must concern himself primarily with the character's reality rather than the audience's experience of his performance.

2 The mechanics of filming require actors to do many technical things to make the shot work.

3 The fragmented nature of shooting means a very different experience for the actor that calls for greater resilience and self-reliance.

The similarities

There are many similarities between what an actor does on screen and on stage. The skills and techniques of preparation and performance, awareness, imagination, empathy, expressivity, physical and vocal dexterity and your ability to work with others and with your nerves – these are all essentials in the actor's toolkit in any medium.

Much of what Stanislavski had to say – circles of attention, inner justification, the magic *if*, objectives and actions, the unbroken line and so on – relates directly to screen work, just as it does to the stage. Uta

Hagen is very much on the money as she describes the imperative to make the character a vivid, three dimensional human being, with a thoroughly fleshed-out past, present and future existence. And Meisner's emphasis on truthful inner life is essential to working on camera.

> Adrian Lester: *'Essentially the job of an actor is the same (on stage and on screen). It's the same imaginative leap, the same honesty. Your truth and application of truth, the moment-to-moment reality, is exactly the same.'*

So your experience to date, the training and all the work you've done to hone your theatre skills are assets and will help you as you set about learning the demands of the new medium.

The differences

At heart, there are only three major differences between acting on the stage and the screen, although all sorts of smaller differences flow from them.

The first and most significant difference lies in the nature of **the relationship between the actor and the audience**. It stems from both the sheer proximity of the camera and the fact that no audience is physically present.

Our interest in dramatic characters is mostly curiosity about their inner worlds. We really want to know how they think and feel in response to the events of the story. On stage, the physical distance between us and the actors means that our only clues are the words and actions. We observe what characters say and do and try to interpret their thoughts and feelings. But the camera comes so close, the character's inner world is accessible to the viewer who can see into his eyes and read his thoughts. Unlike in a theatre, the screen actor has no need to project, and any attempt to do so is immediately exposed as false.

Added to this, there is no audience present during filming to complete the feedback loop through which a stage actor adjusts his performance. True, the director will sometimes give notes between takes, but essentially, the actors are on their own.

This gives rise to a profoundly different relationship between the actor and the audience. I will argue that instead of actively managing how his performance is received, the screen actor should not be giving a performance at all. Rather, he must simply *behave* and allow the camera to share this experience, trusting that the audience will be affected by it.

The second difference is that elements like the photography, sound and design are so central to the screen audience's experience that the **actors are called upon to do many technical things** within the scene, some of which seem alien and wholly artificial.

While it's true that other elements make a contribution in the theatre, the overwhelming majority of the storytelling rests with the actors. But the screen director's bag of tricks is much more extensive and he aims to control pretty much everything the audience experiences. (I can tell you that the director's lot frequently involves deep frustration over the things that one *cannot* control. But that's another story). So an important part of the job is to make the shot work and a screen actor who is not technically adept may flounder.

The third difference lies in **the highly fragmented nature of shooting**. In the theatre the story is told in one continuous stream, with the audience watching the entire drama as it unfolds, from start to finish. The story may be told again the following night, but each time it is created as a single entity. By contrast, the screen story is assembled from numerous tiny morsels, each lasting only a few seconds, painstakingly created in a process that takes weeks, then stitched together in the relative calm of post-production with almost nil input from actors. What the audience actually sees of the actor's performance is decided without his direct involvement.

Together with the absence of an audience and the presence of dozens of technicians, this means a dramatically different *experience* for the actors. There are significantly different demands in terms of concentration, stamina, preparation and focus. It lacks the immediate pay-off of completion and applause but can be deeply rewarding in its mixture of precision and intensity. Some actors hate it, while others find it exhilarating.

These three differences underpin the structure of the book.

Section 1 looks at the relationship between the actor and the audience. It aims to give you an understanding of how screen acting differs from theatre in broad terms, to help you transfer your expertise from stage to screen.

Section 2 examines the technical demands on the actor and functions as a handbook to the practical side of shooting. Some of the techniques it describes can be practised by yourself. But others you will only truly grasp once you start putting them into practice on set, though having an understanding of what will be asked of you, and why, will help you make sense of them. Rereading relevant sections after a day's filming will help consolidate what you learn and hopefully, as you gain more experience you will return to the book and incorporate the more advanced techniques.

And **Section 3** explores how to get, prepare for and do the job. Taking you through from casting to Additional Dialogue Recording (ADR) and the finished product, it aims to prepare you for what to expect and how to do the very best work you can.

SHOWING, SHARING AND THE INNER WORLD

3

SHOWING AND SHARING

On stage you show the audience what your character is experiencing. But the camera comes so close it sees everything and exposes anything fake. Instead of actively communicating with an audience by sending your performance out, your attention needs to be primarily on experiencing the character's reality and sharing it with the camera.

The act of observing changes the thing that's being observed

Imagine you are sitting in a coffee shop talking to someone. The stakes are high as there's something you really want from them. Your attention is focused on your objective: how to get what you want.

Now imagine you become aware of someone at the next table discreetly watching you. You decide not to let on that you know you're being watched. Even though it's a complete stranger and you have no reason to care what he thinks, you can't help being influenced by what you *think* he will think. Even if you decide you don't care what he thinks, you are now engaged in not caring what this unacknowledged observer thinks.

And, of course, this intrusion is sharpened if the observer is someone whose opinion matters to you. You are not only trying to influence the person in front of you, you're also trying to manage the impression you give to the observer. Perhaps you want him to sympathize with you? Perhaps you're keen not to appear dogmatic or unreasonable? Or perhaps, for some other reason, you want him to be intimidated by you? Very subtly, what you say and do will change as you try to achieve two objectives: to get what you want *and* to create the right impression on the observer.

Now imagine that this observer whom you want to influence is much further away. Say, 20 or 30 feet. You have to raise the level of your voice slightly to make sure he hears you. You have to make your facial expressions and gestures just a little more expansive so that what you are doing reads clearly to this distant observer. Where previously you were communicating solely with the person in front of you, you are now communicating both directly with him and indirectly with the person watching.

This difference exists between acting on stage and on screen. The stage actor is in a direct relationship with the audience and has to be active in communicating with it for the simple reason of distance. Even in the smallest studio theatre there will be members of the audience who are a dozen feet away or more. It may not take much adjustment to reach them, but the actor still has to be mindful of their presence and ensure they get the experience they have paid for.

By contrast, the camera can come as close as the director chooses. Almost no matter where it is physically positioned, it can zoom into the tightest close-up (CU). There is no need for the actor to be in a direct relationship with the audience or to communicate actively with it because, via the camera, the audience comes to him. And since the audience isn't even physically present, gauging its response is impossible.

Showing

In the introduction, I referred to the fact that almost all of us come to acting via the stage. From our earliest experience of acting, an integral part of what's going on is that we are giving a performance to people who are watching. We become so accustomed to this state of affairs that we come to think of acting as synonymous with *'performing'* – that is, putting on a show for the benefit of those watching. This is reinforced by some linguistic confusion around the word *'acting'*. To the general public it means pretending or lying. Professional actors, of course, know that acting is actually about telling the truth. After all, what do we mean by *'bad acting'* other than that we don't believe what we're seeing? And yet, most of us probably implicitly consider engaging directly with an audience as inherent in acting. Meisner's greatest contribution to acting was probably a philosophical one. By defining it as *'living truthfully in imaginary circumstances',* he took performance out of the equation.

I described the experience of being watched and of consciously adapting one's behaviour in order to manage the impression one creates. Now let's look at it from the point of view of the observer. Imagine you are watching a man in a railway station who's trying to get his money back from a machine that has swallowed his cash but not given him a ticket. He's infuriated, pressing random buttons vigorously and cursing the machine under his breath. At a given moment he becomes aware that you're watching and starts to feel foolish about conducting an altercation with a machine. So he sighs wearily and rattles the handle as if to say *'this is tiresome but I'm mature enough not to let it get to me'.*

You spot the change: he is no longer living truthfully in the circumstances. Or to be more accurate, he is still living truthfully in circumstances that now include the fact that you are watching. The awareness of this has altered his behaviour. He may not acknowledge that he knows you're watching him, but you see the change in him nonetheless. You might even be able to pinpoint the exact moment when he realizes you're watching, even though he doesn't look at you. He was *being*; now he's *showing*.

The first challenge for stage actors wanting to live truthfully in imaginary circumstances is that it is *really* difficult to be unaffected by the presence of a group of observers. Mark Twain is usually credited with originating the quotation *'dance like no one is watching . . .'*. How many people can truly dance, in front of others, like no one is watching?

We are social animals. We can't help being influenced by the attention of our fellow human beings and wanting to shape how we seem to them. Indeed there's a distinct developmental phase, which begins at around 18 months, during which children become conscious of how they look to the outside eye. By the age of 4, many children have become so acutely self-conscious they can't meet a stranger without hiding behind their parents' legs. We may shed some of this as we grow into adults but we never lose the awareness of how others perceive us. And thank heavens for this, say I. Without it, not only would there be more bad dancing, but we'd be assailed by public nose picking, fashion crimes and the relentless vandalism of uncooperative ticket machines.

The second challenge is that the audience has paid for more than simply to be present while the drama unfolds in a far corner of the room. It wants to witness it, to see and hear what's going on, regardless of where it's sitting. It wants to be moved and entertained. It wants to be included, which means you have to project.

Put together the effect of being watched with the need for projection; throw in the fact that you may be performing the same piece up to eight times a week, and it becomes neither possible nor desirable to behave absolutely as you would if you were not on stage.

Most theatre productions aim for the *'suspension of disbelief'* where the audience temporarily forgets that it's watching actors on a stage and joins in the pretence that the dramatic scenario is actually happening in front of it. Bertolt Brecht explicitly played with the artifice of theatre, deliberately reminding audiences that they were, in fact, watching performances by actors. But even without Brechtian alienation, the most willing suspension of disbelief is only partial. The audience never truly forgets where it is and only ever momentarily loses consciousness of the fact that what it's watching is being staged for its benefit. It's implicit in theatre that the audience is being shown something and it can be overwhelmingly tempting for the stage actor to say to the audience, in effect, *'let me show you what it looks like when my character does or experiences this. . .'*. It's called show business after all.

Even the most eagle-eyed and best-positioned member of a theatre audience does not see the level of detail that is visible on screen. And because the audience knows it is watching actors perform, it seeks a broader, less literal truth.

But precisely because it comes so close, the camera is, in effect, a bullshit-detector that ruthlessly exposes any falsehood. The audience instantly identifies both truthful and untruthful emotion, responding empathetically to the former and rejecting the latter. Certainly anything that smacks of indicating or demonstrating will read as exactly what it is. If we are to believe what we see on screen we demand from the actors a rigorously truthful and spontaneous existence in all its particularities, a much deeper commitment to *'living truthfully in imaginary circumstances'* than is necessary on stage.

To put it bluntly, in the theatre you can generally get away with really clever faking. On screen you generally can't. You could almost go so far as to say that stage acting involves the replication of truths previously discovered in rehearsal. Whereas screen acting involves the spontaneous creation of a truthful inner world during each and every take. And central to the way this plays out in practice is the question of where you put your attention.

Where's your attention?

Go back to the coffee shop example. Before you realize you're being watched, you're wholly focused on whatever it is you're trying to get from the person to whom you're talking. But once you become aware of the observer, your attention is split between managing the impression you're making on him and your original purpose. Your inner monologue has changed.

The inner monologue is so central to the screen actor's craft that it's worth clarifying what I mean by it. Part of the way we make sense of the world is with the help of the little voice in the head that gives us a running commentary on what's going on *out there,* beyond the confines of our own skin, and sometimes about what's happening *in here* – inside our bodies and minds – as well. By silently speaking our thoughts we process what's happening. (And if you think you don't have a little voice in your head, it's the voice that's saying to you *'that's ridiculous, there's no voice in my head, I don't know what he's talking about'*).

TRY IT: To explore the nature of focus of attention try the simple four-step exercise that follows. For it to work, you need to do each step properly, and read the debrief, before moving on to the next step. I have to confess that I'm a terrible cheat when it comes to exercises like this. I almost always read the whole thing through, regardless of what the author says. So please don't be like me. It really will make more sense if you do it step by step. Each instruction ends with the word STOP in capitals and performing all four steps takes only a couple of minutes in total.

Step 1: For 10 seconds, focus all your attention on the word 'stop' at the end of this paragraph. Here it comes: STOP.

Debrief: The likelihood is that your gaze was rooted firmly on the word on the page but perhaps your internal attention wavered between looking at the word and various other uncontrolled thoughts breaking into your inner monologue, such *as: 'What's this about?' 'I wonder if that's ten seconds yet'* and *'Come on, concentrate!'* You may even have found yourself thinking about other things you have to do today or more aware of sounds in the room than you were previously or distracted by something else unconnected with the exercise. All perfectly normal.

Step 2: For 10 seconds, keep your eyes firmly on the word 'stop' at the end of this paragraph, but put your attention on what you can see at the edges of your peripheral vision, working clockwise round your whole field of vision, making a mental note of every item you can see. Here comes the word 'stop': STOP.

Debrief: Assuming you successfully kept your eyes on the word and did the sweep with your peripheral vision, you probably did not find uninvited thoughts invading your inner monologue. Or at least, fewer of them. So even though your eyes were focused on a fixed point, your attention was physically located elsewhere in the room.

Step 3: For 10 seconds keep your eyes firmly on the word 'stop' at the end of this paragraph. Meanwhile recite the alphabet backwards silently in your head. Here comes the word 'stop': STOP.

Debrief: Having a task to do again probably reduced or eliminated the intrusion of uninvited thoughts. And again, even though your eyes were focused on the fixed point on the page, your attention was elsewhere. But this time it didn't have a physical location.

Step 4: For 10 seconds keep your eyes firmly on the word 'stop' at the end of this paragraph. Meanwhile visualize somewhere you know well, perhaps another room in your house or a holiday destination. Here comes the word 'stop': STOP.

Debrief: Whether or not uninvited thoughts intruded, (hopefully) your attention was focused on a physical location other than where you are reading this.

With any luck the steps will have *felt* completely different. And yet, in all four your eyes were simply staring at a point on the page. Our internal attention – what we are actually mentally focusing on – may or may not be related to where our eyes are directed. Thus it's possible to look but not see, to hear but not take in, to taste but not experience.

And what's more, attention is often visible from the outside. A close observer of your eyes, as you did that last exercise, would probably have seen something different in each step. He might not have known *what* you were thinking of but scanning your peripheral vision will probably have looked very different to picturing a holiday destination.

I wrote earlier that one of the fundamental differences between stage and screen acting is to do with the relationship with the audience. The stage actor is implicitly *showing* the audience something. Part of his attention is on the management of how he appears and he makes choices partly for the impact they will have on an observer. The active process of *sending* something out involves effort, however minimal and however well-disguised. On screen this effort is immediately visible and the audience rejects it as being untruthful.

I'm not suggesting that the best stage actors are doing nothing more than demonstrating the character's situation. What's happening is a complex mix of fiction and reality involving pretence, truth, awareness of what comes next, spontaneity, dramatic understanding, consciousness of the audience, performance shtick, execution of technical skills and so on. When it all works, there is a wonderful flow as great stage actors take flight.

But as they do this, part of their attention – knowingly or unknowingly – is engaged in actively communicating with an audience, some of whom are a very long way away at the back of the upper circle. This is necessary and entirely appropriate. But it's also why filmed stage performances – especially when shot in CU – have usually seemed painfully over the top.

An interesting recent development has been theatre productions filmed and broadcast, sometimes live, in cinemas. These are not simply filmed by discrete cameras at the back of the theatre. Rather they are meticulously shot, with cameras dominating the stage foreground in a way that resembles the recording of multi-camera soap operas or *filmed-in-front-of-a-live-audience* sitcoms. The theatre audience knows it is present at a recording and screen viewers never really lose the awareness that what they are watching is a theatre production. The acting is a curious hybrid of stage performances modified for a screen audience and the best of the cast are able to modulate their performances according to the shot, which requires a great degree of technical control.

Don't just do something, stand there

Just as a stage actor cannot dispense with being truthful, neither can a screen actor afford to ignore the camera entirely. He must necessarily make some modifications to *make his inner world available* to the camera, which I will come to later. But there is a distinct philosophical difference between *sending* and *making something available*.

Hugh Bonneville describes the difference as follows: *'On stage you are, by and large, projecting outwards and on camera you are, by and large, inviting an audience in'.* Many successful screen actors talk in similar terms but you may well find yourself thinking *'that's all very well in theory but **how**?'* The answer, especially for actors experienced on stage but inexperienced on screen, involves a leap of faith.

What you need to do, first and foremost, is commit yourself to the fictional reality and trust, *trust* that what you experience will be perceived without you having to push. For actors steeped in the mechanics of theatre, habituated to, and comfortable with, *showing* an audience what is going on, this can feel very risky.

> Juliet Stevenson: *'After 35 years I'm still dragging myself towards trusting the camera enough. You need to do so little. I still often watch myself and am embarrassed by how much I've underestimated the camera. A thought only has to pass through your mind and it registers.'*

Another way of thinking about this is the difference between convex and concave. The convex bulges outwards, while the concave curves inwards. By this analogy, a stage performance is convex, pushing something out to the audience, whereas a screen performance is concave, drawing the audience's attention towards it.

The direct communication with the audience is something that many stage actors miss when working on screen, because filming deprives you of this immediate feedback and the certainty of knowing your impact.

There are people present while you're filming of course – the other actors and the crew – but they have a very different relationship with the material and with you. They are also mostly standing 10 to 20 feet away, just like a theatre audience, whereas the camera may be in a tight CU. So their response may not be the same as the audience's when the footage is cut together. It's true, for example, that just because the crew finds something funny doesn't mean the audience will. And vice versa.

The actor who pitches his performance to appeal to those present on set is on the road to overacting. Apart from whatever you're asked to do technically to make the shot work, your attention needs to be focused entirely on the fictional reality and your character's inner world.

This is actually not so different from Stanislavski's dictum that the actor's point of attention should be *this* side of the stage lights, rather than in the auditorium. Yet, 80 years after he was writing, stage actors who ignore this advice are still depressingly common.

Does any actor ever truly forget that he's actually pretending to be someone else? I doubt it. All acting requires the actor to hold two realities simultaneously: the actual and the fictional. We can't really do this, of course, any more than we can simultaneously scan our peripheral vision *and* visualize a holiday destination. The closest we can come is to alternate our attention between them rapidly and for the skilled actor it's probably more accurate to say that there's a messy, indefinable blur between the two realities – the character's and the actor's own – with the balance between them in constant flux.

At moments of deepest emotion, the really committed actor may fleetingly lose his consciousness that the circumstances are imaginary, that he's *acting,* and be absorbed into the character's reality. At moments that are technically demanding – during a fight scene for example – the actor's reality may be uppermost with thoughts like *'don't actually stab the other guy'* dominating.

The theatre insists the actor give weight to both the fictional reality *and* the actual reality (the audience's experience) and the starting point for a stage performance is a triangular relationship with the other actor and the audience. The starting point on screen is a two-way relationship: just you and the other actor. The camera's greater access and proximity-derived bullshit-detection requires us to focus much more deeply on the fictional – the imaginary circumstances, other characters and our own character's experience – from the inside. And what dominates the consciousness of a character, just like any real person, is their inner world.

4
THE INNER WORLD

Most of our experience is unspoken and internal. When we look closely at others we are highly sophisticated at reading faces and this is what the camera enables the viewer to do: to see into the inner world. Screen acting is as much about reacting as acting.

The close-up and the inner monologue

Because the theatre audience is sitting on the other side of the room – and sometimes it's a very large room indeed – it can only infer what's going on internally for the characters from what they say, how they say it and any physical movements that are large enough to be seen from the auditorium.

In his lectures and writing on story structure, Robert McKee argues that the territory of the novel is the intra-personal – the individual's inner world. Theatre, he says, deals best with the inter-personal – the relationships between individuals. And the forte of film and television is the extra-personal – the relationship between an individual and the environment or society.

While that may be true for the story themes, the camera gives us access to the inner monologue and it's the actor, not the author, who writes that script. Only a tiny fraction of what we experience results in speech and the close-up (CU) enables us to see behind the words, right into the character's soul, penetrating his innermost thoughts and emotions as he suffers the slings and arrows of outrageous fortune. Creating and inhabiting a rich and vibrant inner world is one of the primary tasks of the actor. And audience access to this inner world is one of most profound differences between stage and screen.

When we pay close attention to others – when we *really* look and *really* listen, as the CU allows us to – we are incredibly perceptive. Malcolm Gladwell coined the phrase *'thin-slicing'* to describe the ability people develop, after many years of experience, to assess and understand something deeply at a glance, without conscious thought. Gladwell applies it to seasoned professionals like art experts who can tell at a glance whether a painting is genuine. But when it comes to reading people's faces and understanding subtext, we can all thin-slice because we've been doing it since we were tiny babies.

We can see thoughts. We register the tiniest flicker of emotion in the face or voice. In particular, we look at the eyes which are staggeringly expressive. When people's eye movements are tracked as they look at a face, the result is a triangle from eye to eye, down to the mouth and back up to the eyes. And of this, the most attention is paid to the eyes. The musculature around them is enormously complicated and emotions are directly expressed in them, many involuntarily, as Paul Ekman's research demonstrates. Similarly, when we can hear the voice clearly and naturally, with all its nuance of intonation and without the projection required in the theatre, we are capable of detecting the subtlest shades of feeling. Of course, as we watch a film we are not remotely interested in how all this happens. We just read a character's face, listen to his voice and divine what he is thinking and feeling.

A CU on screen is like watching someone's face, with 100 per cent of your attention, from just a few inches away. In life, the only people who scrutinize another human being this closely are mothers with newborn babies and new lovers as they strain to explore each other's inner world. (And it's debatable whether lovers really are interested in their partner's inner world, or whether they just want an answer to the question *'what do you think of* **me***?'*)

There are two reasons why we don't generally look this closely in real life: (1) we are too wrapped up in our own experience – our own inner world – to be sufficiently interested in others and (2) it involves a degree of intimacy that is almost painful and therefore generally taboo. However, one of the great joys of story is that it enables us temporarily to let go of our own cares and concerns and empathize with the struggles of somebody else. And somehow the screen beguiles us into believing that what we are watching is real, or at least more real than what goes on on stage.

Logically this makes no sense. If we were watching real life we wouldn't be able to change our viewpoint the way the camera does. There's also a complex interplay between our knowing that this is a drama, our recognition of famous actors, our non-recognition of actors we've never seen before, and so on. For example, we know that the famous actor's character can't disappear from the story in the first few minutes: even if they die, they'll re-enter the narrative in flashback or imagination or as a ghost or somehow. But aside from this, while we are watching we don't consciously make any of these calculations. What we are seeing just *feels* more real than it does when we are in a theatre. And yet, simultaneously, we understand that the characters don't see us, so the intimacy taboo is not breached.

For the audience then, what's happening internally, behind the character's eyes, is as interesting as what he does externally. Where the stage actor concerns himself with action, the screen actor's focus is as much on *reaction* as action. And this is largely about listening.

5
LISTENING

Listening is often more important than speaking. Listening is about trying to figure out what's happening in the other character's inner world and saying your lines to affect this.

Listening and the inner world

Of all the elements that make up an actor's performance on screen, listening is one of the most fundamental. It's also an inversion, in many cases, of what happens in the theatre, where speaking is the thing. Whether they admit it or not, stage actors initially assess their parts on the basis of what they get to say: *How many lines do I have?* A student of mine recently complained that there is no male character in the scene I had asked him to prepare for the next class. I pointed out that there is, he just doesn't speak. *'Oh great'* he grumbled, completely missing the point that the internal reactions of the character – whose wife has been brain-damaged in giving birth to a child that then died – were potentially more interesting than either of the speaking characters.

In the theatre we tend to follow the dialogue by watching the speaker, only occasionally glancing at the listener. So, from an actor's perspective, the speakers drive the scene and command the attention. Words = glory. However, on screen, a well-written and well-edited scene will often focus more on the listener.

There are often critical moments in exchanges when we understand what is being said and the question of how it lands with the listener becomes more interesting than what's happening for the speaker. A well-edited piece will cut to the listener at precisely this moment. If we look carefully – and this is as true in life as it is in drama – in this split-second we will see an open and unguarded response on the face of the listener that reveals his true feelings. Thin-slicing enables us to read the person's inner world.

It only lasts a microsecond before he manages his external response to show what he wants to show. This, too, is something we all do once we get past the age of about 7 or 8. We know the person in front of us may be watching and we're just endeavouring to get what we want (which includes coming across in the way we want to come across). It's not really about deception or insincerity, it's just another manifestation of the fact that being observed changes our behaviour. Think how differently you respond to significant news you hear over the phone, alone, compared with news that is told to you face to face, or even over the phone when other people are present.

As an aside, it's one of the reasons small children are so compelling to watch. They have not yet learnt to mask their feelings and what you see is what you get. Hence the advice never to act with children and animals: their openness means they're likely to be more interesting than you.

Given all this, the tempting thing might be to choreograph your responses to key moments within a scene, either as part of your preparation or from one take to another. But this takes us right back into the territory of showing. In effect, what you will be doing is showing the audience what it looks like when someone experiences this moment. And because the camera comes so incredibly close, it sees into your soul and it knows when you are lying.

I'm not suggesting that a highly technically skilled actor cannot make a pretty good fist of mimicking a truthful response. The audience may not even be aware that this is what the actor is doing. But these are not the moments that truly move us. These are not the moments that grip our hearts and make us weep with laughter or sympathy. Moments like this come from an intense identification with a human being who is undergoing a vivid personal experience and this is what the audience wants to see: somebody living truthfully in imaginary circumstances.

Directors and editors spend weeks in the cutting room, crawling painstakingly through the footage looking for these moments, selecting a few frames from one take and a few frames from another. It's what drives the decision to feature one actor more than another in the cut.

When faced with a scene between one actor who is relentlessly delivering these moments of truth and another who is just faking their way through a scene, you play most of the scene on the former, regardless of how many lines they have. Indeed, I remember saying to an editor, when faced with a problem moment in a scene, *'let's cut to X, there is always something interesting going on there'*. What I meant was that X had a vivid inner life.

Michael Caine tells a lovely story about being a young actor on stage with very few lines of dialogue. When asked by the director what his character says in response to what's happening in the scene, Caine replied that his character has nothing to say. Wrong, said the director, your character has hundreds of things to say. He just chooses not to say them.

But, truth be told, however absorbed in events he was as he sat at the side of the stage, he was unlikely to command the audience's attention because he was too far away for them to see clearly how he was affected by what he heard. Unless he projected.

Film the scene in close-up (CU), however, and things are different. And this is a lesson that Caine has turned into a glittering career. On screen, a really vivid inner life will win out over bluster and projection, however well executed. I know I ought to say that acting is not a competition – and of course it isn't, it's really about creative collaboration – but it's a rare actor who does not want the audience's attention. And on screen, this means screen time.

> **Juliet Stevenson:** *'On stage you've only got body language and the line. Nothing you 'think' is going to reach anyone in the stalls in a 3,000 seater.'*

So, if contriving our responses does not work, what should we do? The answer is both simple and incredibly complex: *listen*. The actor who is truly open and truly listening will respond internally to everything that is going on in the scene. Listening is absolutely central to generating a vivid inner life.

You've probably heard before how important listening is to acting. You may, like me as a young actor, have found your attention wavering uncontrollably. Or, perhaps you have stood there, committed to listening, but dimly aware that instead of *actually* listening to the other person you're really listening to that voice in your head that's telling you to *'listen, damn you, listen'*.

Point of attention

How does one listen? What does it actually entail? To understand better, it's useful to have a clear understanding of what's involved in consciousness and for this, it's necessary to come back to Stanislavski's notion of *point of attention.*

I wrote earlier about the need for actors to keep as much of their attention as possible on the character's reality, rather than on their own reality – that of the actor in the drama. Some older actors deploy a technique for avoiding corpsing, which is to look at the eyebrows of the person to whom they're speaking, instead of their eyes. Corpsing is actors laughing about something in their reality, not the character's reality. So if you don't look in the other actor's eyes, you don't make the actor-to-actor connection that can set this off. And it works. If you don't connect you are indeed much less likely to corpse. But of course, it also means the characters don't connect either. Instead, the actor is working in a self-contained bubble, delivering his performance as planned, with minimal input from what's going on around him.

So the first thing you must do is to forget about this kind of bullshit, whether on stage or screen, and commit yourself to the dramatic reality – the *here-and-now* of the scene.

Assuming you succeed in doing this, there are still two primary places your (character's) point of attention can be. The first is what I referred to earlier as *out there,* focused on what's going on around you and seeking information. The second is *in here*, the inner world. *In here* is where the inner monologue takes place as we talk to ourselves, processing what's going on *out there,* considering how it affects us and impacts on our hopes and dreams and fears. The traffic between *out there* and *in here* defines our engagement with the world, as our attention alternates between the external and the internal.

Listening is not just about having our point of attention *out there* in the world outside ourselves. It's about specifically having it *over there* – focused on the person with whom we're interacting and engaged in what I call *'the act of enquiry'* – trying to figure out what they want and mean – and allowing it to affect us *in here*. And it's surprisingly difficult to do. This is true in life as well as when we are acting. It requires us to be truly present, in the *here-and-now*, profoundly open to, and influenced by, what's in front of us. It's all too easy in life, while the other guy is talking, to do listening behaviour – nodding and smiling and grunting *'uh huh'* – to indicate that we are listening, while internally we rehearse what we're going to say when he stops talking. There is no act of enquiry. There is merely speaking and waiting to speak.

You will almost certainly have been on the receiving end of this. You'll have had the experience of sensing, just *sensing*, that the person you're talking to isn't really listening, despite the fact that they're doing plenty of listening behaviour. It's particularly common at parties, especially where there's networking to be done. Someone asks how you are and, while you explain about your recent haemorrhoid operation, you just know that, despite making all the right listening noises, he's really scanning the room for someone more important/interesting/sexy to talk to.

And how many of us have been caught out by a partner on the phone, reading the newspaper or typing an email while pretending to listen?

                    PARTNER
        So you'll never guess what he said then.

                      YOU
            (typing)

        Go on.

                    PARTNER
        You're not listening to me.

                      YOU
            (withdrawing hands hurriedly
            from the keyboard)
        Yes I am!

How did he/she know? In fact it's easy: something tiny was askew in the way you said *'go on'*; some nuance in the timing just wasn't quite right. We *know* when someone is not listening to us; we can just tell.

And this is just with a voice over the phone. When you add in a real, live human being, with the particular potency of eye contact, it's even more apparent whether someone is listening to us or not.

The theatre audience, watching a conversation between two characters but seated tens of feet away, can't always tell the difference between expertly faked listening and the real thing. But the screen audience – looking deep into the actor's eyes, remember – knows absolutely when an actor is engaged in listening, heart and soul, and when they are simply doing listening acting.

In life, being listened to is compelling. When someone really and truly gives us their wholehearted attention, it is special and deeply gratifying. It's also worth mentioning that it's often highly charismatic. People used to say of the actor Vincent Price that when he shook your hand it felt as though he had crossed the Atlantic just to say hello to you. I've heard similar comments made about Barack Obama and many other charismatic leaders. You might think they have a lot going on and will be preoccupied by other things, but instead, they focus all their attention on you. They really want to know what you think, and it's devastatingly charming, especially when compared with the preening narcissism of some celebrities.

So when it comes to listening on screen there's something profoundly important about genuinely placing your point of attention on the other person. If you want a really good example of this, watch Ryan Gosling in *The Place Beyond the Pines* or Michael Fassbender in *12 Years a Slave*. Both have moments of extraordinarily intense listening that is utterly compelling.

But what are we listening *for* as we engage in the act of enquiry?

Harold Pinter knew a thing or two about the relationship between words and the inner life. In his magnificent essay *The Echoing Silence* he dissects how we use words, not to communicate and reveal, but to cover our uncertainty. The real communication takes place in the silence between words.

This profound understanding of the relationship between speech and silence is what made him such a great screenwriter as well as playwright. And what he's writing about is not acting, but life. More remains unsaid than is said. Clint Eastwood – a master of screen silence – and the wordless Michael Caine on stage are still living a vivid inner life. When you really listen to someone else, you engage with this. It's not about the words so much as what's *behind* the words. You try to figure out what he is *really* saying, what he is *not* saying, what is *really* going on for him.

The Chinese character 'to listen' (Figure 1) combines the ideas of listening with the ears and the heart: giving the whole of one's undivided attention. And this is what an actor needs to bring to his listening.

Now, of course, it's not just the other person who has an inner world. So do you. And so does your character. I have already suggested that, as far as possible, you must let go of your – the actor's – inner world. The inner monologue must be the character's, not the actor's. Your character's inner world is what we're really interested in. What you say and do hints at it, but – and this is one of the glorious possibilities of screen acting – through your eyes we can divine so much more. Listening involves internal changes in **you** in response to what you hear and see. The *over there* – what the other character says and does – affects the *in here* – what you think and feel.

Alan Alda, who won 21 Emmys between 1972 and 1983 for acting, writing and directing on the series M*A*S*H, describes listening like this: *'When I started out as an actor, I thought "here's what I have to say; how shall I say it?" On M*A*S*H I began to understand what I do in this scene is not as important as what happens between me and the other person. And listening is what lets it happen. It's almost always the other person who causes you to say what you say next. You don't have to figure out how you say it. You have to listen so simply, so innocently, that the other person brings about a change in you that makes you say it and informs the way you say it.'*

TO LISTEN

ear

one heart (ie: undivided attention)

Figure 1 To listen.

I love this. He goes on to describe listening as *'a willingness to let the other person change you'*. This, I think, goes to the very heart of the matter, both in life and acting. If you are not open to being changed, you're not listening. You're just pausing while the other person speaks.

And listening is not restricted to the moments when the other person is talking. Even as you deliver your lines in the script, they will be having an impact on the other character(s) in the scene. If you keep looking and listening, you will see subtle, and sometimes not so subtle, changes in the other person. In life, these changes affect what you say and how you say it. This must, MUST influence what you do in a scene in just the same way, even though the words (and some actions) are predetermined. You must be willing to let the other person change you.

> **Hugh Bonneville:** *'The most damaging thing is to be utterly assured before you arrive on set about how you're going to do it, because that leaves no room for being alive to what the other actor might bring to the scene.'*

Of course the danger is that the more you rehearse the scene, the more you know not just how your fellow actors will say their lines but how you will respond. So it becomes harder to continue to listen, to remain willing to let the other person change you. But the moment you stop really, truly listening – being influenced by what's *over there* – the screen audience will know it. They will detect that you are not experiencing a truthful internal response to what is going on in the scene and that you are ACTING. And they will no longer believe you.

If you truly engage, as your character, with the other characters in the scene, and they truly engage with you, it will be different every time you play the scene and it will be electric. The lines may be the same but if you really listen you will detect micro differences in the other character's inner world. And by 'listen', technically I mean put your attention on the intonation, speed, volume, the expression in the eyes, the movements, gestures and so on. But really I mean put your attention on what's behind the words, the intention underlying them and what's not being said. The micro differences in your *over there* will change what happens to your *in here* and give rise to similar micro differences in what you do and how you deliver your lines.

Spontaneity

You can't plan this. Sir Ben Kingsley uses the analogy of a tennis ball coming over the net. You can't decide to play a forehand on the next shot because you don't know where the ball is going to land. You simply hit the ball back as it comes to you.

This is a fantastic metaphor for screen acting. You can plan all you like – and I'm a big believer in actors doing lots of preparation – but in the moment of the take you have to respond to what is coming at you. Laurence Olivier was getting at the same thing when he advised a young actress that if she thought she'd found the right inflection, not to use it. It's about the *'unbroken flow'* that Stanislavski writes of. Without it, you have nothing but posturing and showing off and the camera sees right through it.

> Sir Ben Kingsley: '*The camera will not tolerate acting. On-screen you must be. I am no longer engaged in acting, I'm engaged in being.*'

> Hugh Bonneville: '*Acting is reacting. You can only be as alive in a scene as the other actor allows you to be. And if you give a pre-packaged performance, you're doing your fellow actor a disservice and ultimately you're doing the scene a disservice. There has to be the electricity that is created by dialogue between actors, spoken and unspoken, creating a third thing, which is the scene.*'

A couple of thoughts here about Michael Caine's brilliant television masterclass on screen acting. Caine has had a long, illustrious career. He is a superb technician who truly understands how to work on camera. He also has much of interest to say about the actor's process and I cite or quote him several times in this book. But where I profoundly disagree with him is when he describes not needing the other actor to read his lines when he is doing his CU. He talks about how the other actor can go home as he, Caine, can deliver his lines to the wall, if necessary.

To my mind there is little as exciting as the tension generated when two characters really connect on a deep level. What this requires from the actors, above all else, is vulnerability and finding this in the middle of the technical circus that is filming is not easy. But I would argue that it's essential if you are to move an audience.

The truth is there is no right way of doing this thing called 'acting'. There are many ways of approaching it and it's probably true to say that there is a spectrum running from Caine at one end – technically brilliant but often very self-contained – through to someone like Ben Kingsley at the other end, who is profoundly connected.

As you'll see, what I'm advocating is much closer to Kingsley's approach.

Meryl Streep: *'It's not about the audience. It's all about fooling the other actors into believing who you say you are. . . . I take my entire performance from them, so if they don't look at me and hate me appropriately or love me the way they're supposed to . . . then I'm lost, I don't have anything to go on.'*

Juliet Stevenson: *'What a camera records is what's going on between people, how they are affecting and influencing other people. . . . No human being is shaped by just themselves. Connect with each other.'*

6

COMMITMENT

Unreserved commitment to the fictional reality, from the moment you hear 'action', is vital for screen actors. You can train yourself to commit in your life as well as your work. It's essential to banish embarrassment.

Creating the imaginary world

In the theatre, there is a collective imagination at work that supports and reinforces the actors' imaginations. When you walk onto the stage, you walk into a bubble where not only the cast, but the entire audience is committed to sustaining the make-believe that the world is that of the drama. This fictional world has clear boundaries: it exists in a pool of light and once you set foot on the stage, you are your character. As soon as you step back into the wings, you re-enter the real world where other actors and stage managers talk to you as *you*, rather than in the persona of your character. If an actor has to take a prompt, it jars and the audience and actors alike are relieved when the play is resumed. If another actor speaks to you onstage, outside the drama, actor-to-actor, it jars even if it's too quiet for the audience to hear. It can occasionally feel thrillingly naughty for that very reason: it is breaking the spell.

On a film set the only people wholly emotionally invested in the imaginary world are the actors. The director will occasionally come to visit, but much of his time is spent managing and directing the mechanics of shooting. Unlike in a theatre, you are hugely outnumbered by people whose concern is practical tasks. The lighting and camera teams concern themselves with the picture. The boom operator and sound recordist are only really interested in capturing the sound. The assistant directors just want the shoot to run smoothly and to time. And so on. The art department probably comes closest through its effort to create a three-dimensional story world, but even the art director is not concerned with the emotional exchange between the fictional characters.

It's not that they don't understand the dramatic setting. Most of them are talented and creative artists. But only you and the director are directly concerned with the emotional landscape. And living truthfully in it is your department, not theirs.

Unlike on stage the boundaries to this imaginary world are often fuzzy, with partial sets or walls taken out and put back in. Many drama schools use some variation of Uta Hagen's object exercises so you may have direct experience of the power of objects to help create imaginary reality. And yet, on a set this reality is constantly violated as technicians trample in and out of the story world with objects and equipment that don't belong there. You too may well be asked to float in and out, delivering your off-camera lines from the gloomy fringes of the lighting to an actor who is pretending he can see you clearly.

There is an internal quality that enables the best actors to create a character with a vivid and truthful inner world in such a partially constructed external world: **commitment**.

Commitment

Along with listening, commitment is probably the most important thing a screen actor brings to his performance and is the quality a director looks for the most.

The kind of commitment I'm talking about is an absolute acceptance of the fictional reality without hesitation, embarrassment or inhibition. The playwright Anthony Nielson describes watching John Malkovich in a rehearsed reading, many years ago, during which his character had to answer the phone. With no prop Malkovich lifted his fist, sticking out his thumb and little finger to represent the receiver. Nielson makes the point that most actors would have quickly realized that they looked ridiculous and were guilty of doing *'bad phone acting'*. Surreptitiously they would have adjusted their hand to a less embarrassing position. Malkovich, however, simply committed himself to his choice and not for a split second did Nielson see this waver.

Total commitment is the hallmark of the great actor, whatever the medium. Unfortunately, a combination of the airy distractions of the theatre, the need to project, perhaps the fatigue and predictability of repeated performances and, sadly quite often, complacency means that these moments are rare. And sometimes, to be less harsh, a stage actor's intense commitment can go unnoticed because the audience is just too far away.

Committing at the beginning of a take is often particularly problematic for inexperienced screen actors. But you cannot afford to take even a few seconds to get up to speed. The analogy with jumping off a diving board is hardly original, but there are definitely similarities for me with the childhood experience of sitting around on the top board of the local swimming pool, with several other boys, all trying to pluck up the courage to jump. Occasionally you would go and peer over the edge and confirm to yourself that it was, indeed, a very long way down. Eventually I learnt that the only way to jump was not to look down, but simply to walk towards the edge and launch myself without hesitating.

Adrian Lester: *'In a play, losing yourself within a flow is the key because one moment drives the next and so on. You can get lost in that flow, so that you come up for air two hours later and it's the end. On screen you don't get the chance to do that. But as soon as somebody shouts 'action' you have to be in the middle of the same kind of flow as you would have been onstage – just lost within it.'*

I firmly believe this kind of commitment can be learnt, or at least intensified. It's undoubtedly true that some actors just have it. They seem able to commit themselves, absolutely and effortlessly, without any internal struggle or complications. This is one of the qualities that stars often have from the very beginning. Lucky them. For the rest of us, training ourselves to commit in everything we do is a central part of the struggle to become better actors.

It's at the core of what drama schools attempt to teach. There is often a moment when an actor becomes 'trained'; when everything seems to fall into place and they 'get it'. Thereafter there may still be technical things to be learnt and improvements to be made, but fundamentally, the major work of training has been done.

The most stark example of this that I've seen was when working with the street-dance group Diversity in preparation for a movie. Being dancers, these guys live in their bodies and have far fewer difficulties with thinking obstructing feeling than, say, your average graduate student at drama school. This is not to say the members of Diversity are not smart. They're bright guys, some of whom are educated to degree level. But their intelligence is physical and emotional as much as intellectual. They also, of course, commit. A dancer who doesn't commit has nothing.

There was a particular moment with one of the group, when he and I re-enacted a significant moment from his past. He improvised things that he had wanted to say at the time but been unable to, and it was as if a dam burst. Out it all came – the anger and frustration and disappointment and hurt – and something clicked. From then on, in every scripted scene we rehearsed, he absolutely committed and rapidly became a very good actor indeed.

This kind of commitment doesn't only happen when we act. It can exist as we go about our everyday lives. There will always be times when we feel uncertain or indecisive. But we can train ourselves to push past this. And sport, again, provides a useful comparison because top sports men and women commit. It's what they must do if they are to win.

A famous example was provided by the 1968 Olympics men's 200 m medal ceremony. It was at the height of the civil rights movement in the United States – the struggle by black Americans for equality – and African-American sprinters Tommie Smith and John Carlos had finished first and third, respectively. They had been warned by the Olympic authorities not to make any kind of political protest when receiving their medals. But both wore black gloves at the ceremony and raised a fist in the Black Power salute as soon as the Star Spangled Banner began to play (Figure 2).

© PA Images

Figure 2 Commitment.

What's particularly interesting is the difference in their physicality at this moment of immense courage. Carlos, who came from the Harlem ghetto in New York, was generally perceived to be the more fiery character, whereas Smith, a Texan, was described as more placid. But Smith is the more upright. His arm is straighter and his entire body language suggests unconditional conviction. Whereas Carlos's arm is bent and his body language conveys something hesitant and uncertain. Now, I am no expert on athletics, but I strongly believe that our bodies and voices express our inner lives. And what I see in their bodies is different levels of commitment.

Both men were clearly hugely talented and dedicated athletes and what they did was incredibly brave. The following year, despite being suspended from the US team and receiving death threats, Carlos broke the world record. But what is it that distinguishes performances between world-class athletes? I suspect the reason that Smith was the victor in 1968 was to do, above everything else, with commitment. And that commitment manifested itself in his body during the medal ceremony as well as during the race.

The greatest actors share a similar ability to commit to the exclusion of all else and, because the camera comes so very close, this facility is particularly important to screen actors.

To illustrate my point that this kind of commitment is something that can exist in any area of life, let me offer another example taken from sport, but one that comes from the stands, not the field of play.

I recently went to see Chelsea play Napoli in the European Champions' League. The Napoli fans' chanting was extraordinary: intense, ferocious and astonishingly well-coordinated. As I looked closer I spotted the general who was orchestrating this. Throughout the game he barely glanced at the game on the pitch. Instead he faced his own supporters and conducted them. Bare-chested on a cold March night, with every fibre of his being he was wholly and utterly committed to one thing only: inciting passion in the Napoli fans. It was mesmerizing to watch.

Many of the greatest screen performances are driven by this kind of ferocious commitment. A fantastic example is Sir Ben Kingsley's portrayal of Don in *Sexy Beast*. Ray Winstone – who plays Gal, the retired gangster whom Don attempts to bully into doing one last job – is reputed to have been amused at the idea that he could be intimidated by the actor who played Gandhi. Yet, the physically slight Kingsley is terrifyingly intense as Don, especially in the very scene where he browbeats Gal.

Commitment like this has ramifications not just for your work but also for your whole engagement with the world. When you do something, do it for real. Practise committing yourself to whatever you are doing. Practise overcoming self-doubt. Practise ignoring any self-consciousness or embarrassment by pushing through it. Embarrassment is the enemy of good acting, so never, *ever* let it stop you doing something. This really is something you can train yourself to do. Like Alan Alda performing a cartwheel, get better at identifying your own impulses and recognizing when embarrassment is preventing you from following through.

It's quite likely that some appetite for exhibitionism drove you to become an actor in the first place. Celebrate this and develop it in yourself. Exhibitionism for its own sake can be pretty wearing for those in the vicinity and I'm not suggesting you relentlessly show off just for the sake of showing off. But any hint of embarrassment or inhibition in your screen performance will be glaringly obvious on camera and you absolutely need to cultivate the ability to banish it.

SECTION TWO

MAKE THE SHOT WORK

7
FILMING – THE BIG PICTURE

Actors are primarily only involved in production – the middle of the three stages of filming. Production is incredibly expensive so actors must help meet the schedule by adjusting their performances technically.

Development (and pre-pre-production)

There are really five phases to the entire process of creating a screen work. While the first two do not need to concern actors much, it's worth having an awareness of them.

Development is the name given to the period before actual physical production begins. It involves writing the script, attaching the director and assembling the finance, which itself is usually dependent on securing the commitment of star actors. Development is the really cheap part as it mostly involves only ideas on paper. It's also probably the most important – if you get the script right, everything that follows becomes easier. Or at least if you *don't* get the script right, everything that follows is doomed as you try to make a silk purse from a sow's ear.

You'll also sometimes hear producers talk about *pre*-pre-production, which is the phase before pre-production officially begins and money is released. This involves recruiting the key players and putting the major elements in place but before people start getting paid.

Producers live in a state of perpetual optimism and, in some cases, self-delusion. Hundreds of projects are in development for every one that actually gets made and dozens never make it from *pre*-pre-production into production.

There's a not-terribly-funny joke that goes *'how do you know when a producer is lying?'* to which the answer is *'because his lips are moving'*. It reflects the desperation with which producers, and often directors, particularly ones at the start of their careers, will try to galvanize a project into being. Their zeal can lead them to use the term *'pre-production'* pretty flexibly. A project that's described as being in pre-production may well actually be in pre-pre-production or even development, that is, they're still trying to get the money together.

Most of what I'll describe assumes a fully funded production for television or film. But there is also a cottage industry in most countries of low-budget indie films, including short films, financed by the producer or the director or their uncle or lover or someone who's made a lot of money elsewhere and wants to get into films. These range from the no-hope affairs of fantasists that will never see the light of day, through to the early projects of people who will go on to become world-famous producers and directors. They all offer you the valuable chance to practise working on camera. But if you're cast in a low-budget, indie film project, especially if you're beginning to acquire a bit of a name as an actor, you'd be wise to take what you're told about start dates with a pinch of salt.

If you are asked to be in a film that's in development or pre-pre-production, and you have an agent, they'll be able to bring some realism to the assessment of what's going on. If not, don't go out and spend your anticipated fee, even if they tell you it's fully financed. I don't want to give the impression that all producers are out and out liars. But it is genuinely very difficult to get any film made without at least bending the truth. There's never any malice involved – they're just young hustlers trying to give some momentum to a cherished project on which they've worked, unpaid, for years. But they can often be careless with the feelings and enthusiasm of those they involve. Once people start being paid, you know things are serious.

If, on the other hand, you're seen for a part in, say, a television series being made by a reputable production company, you're on much more solid ground. That's not to say things can't change – dates get put back, stars pull out and the production is put on hold, etc. – but you can be fairly confident things will be above board.

Three phases of production

In order to understand the technical demands on the actor and the experience of filming it's helpful to appreciate the practical, and particularly the financial context.

There are three distinct phases to production once a project has been green-lit that is, approved for production by whoever's putting up the money:

1 pre-production
2 production
3 post-production

Pre-production

This involves everything that goes on prior to the first day of shooting: all the logistics, including hiring the personnel and equipment, finding and setting up the locations, the hugely complicated business of scheduling, right through to organizing the catering. The only involvement in this that most actors will see is a few minutes in the casting process when they meet the director and/or the casting director. And, depending on the size of the production – whether it is television or film, and so on – there will probably be a wardrobe fitting and a readthrough.

But other than that, the actor will usually have no contact with anyone (other than a phone call or two about logistical arrangements) until his first day of shooting. Meanwhile all sorts of decisions that will directly affect him are taken by other people. Sets will be designed and built, props chosen, costume, hair and make-up choices get made. There will probably be some script changes. But however busy this period – and it is incredibly busy for the director particularly – it's relatively cheap, as only a fairly small number of people are on the payroll at this point.

Post-production

This involves everything that takes place once the shoot has finished and it is also relatively inexpensive. The footage is edited, sound mixed, picture graded, score composed and soundtrack created before the finished product is finally delivered to the paymasters – the broadcaster or distributor. Again the actor's involvement in this is minimal, usually no more than a few minutes (or possibly hours, depending on the size of your part) recording a few lines of dialogue in a sound studio, either because there is a problem with what was recorded during the shoot or new, off-camera dialogue is needed. There are several names for this but in the United Kingdom it is most commonly known as ADR (Additional Dialogue Recording). There might also occasionally be a day or two of further shooting: either a couple of extra shots, or even an additional, freshly written scene, because something in the story is unclear. In extreme circumstances there may even be a reshoot of an unsatisfactory scene.

Production

This is the part of the process in which actors are integrally involved. However, it's important to understand that you are only a very small element of shooting. Personally I would argue that actors are the second most important element after the script – if the story is well structured and the performances are good, the audience will accept inferior photography, design, sound and everything else. But then I would say that, wouldn't I? The sound recordist would argue that if you can't hear the dialogue, it doesn't matter how good the script is. The Director of Photography (DoP) would tell you that the photography is the primary means of telling the story. The designer would insist that without an intelligent and beautifully realized setting, there is no world in which the characters can exist. And so on through the other creative departments.

And all of them are right. Because filming is a collaborative process between many creative people and the acting, while vital, is not the sole focus of the shoot. As in pretty much all aspects of life, money is what really drives the decision-making. And on a film set, almost everything is geared towards making the most efficient use of money. This is not to say a film set is always efficient, but it's what everyone is striving for.

The average crew consists of 30 to 40 people, in addition to the director, so filming is hugely expensive. There are a lot of wages involved and the moment the unit goes into overtime, it's very, *very* costly. Consequently, the efficient use of time is fundamental to everyone's jobs, including the cast's. This means that if the director is going to wind up pleased that he hired you – and therefore consider you again next time he is casting and recommend you to his friends – you had better do your bit to help the shoot run smoothly and efficiently: **make the shot work**.

Meeting the schedule

The most immediate measure of whether things are working efficiently or not (and the one the financiers are watching like hawks) is whether the schedule is met. To understand why this is so important consider the consequences of **not** meeting the schedule in a particular location. That location will only have been booked for the minimum number of days because hiring locations is expensive. Additional personnel and expensive bits of kit may only have been booked for those days. And the actors whose scenes take place in that location may only have been booked for a few days. So to return to that location, whether it's the next day or later in the schedule, is very expensive and has knock-on implications for the rest of the shoot. Even if, either by chance or prophetic scheduling, it is possible to return to the same location the following day, the unit then has to travel to the next location during a shooting day. A production unit, comprising upwards of 30 people as well as at least a dozen lighting wagons, camera trucks, generators, make-up and wardrobe wagons, trailers, catering wagons and so on, does not move quickly. To move half a mile will take a minimum of 2 hours and, by definition, time spent travelling between locations is wasted filming time. And wasted filming time is wasted money. Even if the entire shoot is based in a studio, not meeting the schedule is very likely to have serious consequences for the production and especially the director.

Once you understand that meeting the schedule drives the decision-making, all sorts of other peculiarities in the mechanics of shooting, that make little or no sense from the actor's point of view, start to look comprehensible. For example, scenes are almost invariably shot out of story order. Scenes that take place in the same location will be shot back to back, regardless of where they come in the story. Because moving the entire production unit from one location to another is so incredibly costly, it makes no financial sense to use the location on two different days, when both scenes can be shot on the same day. So you may find yourself shooting a scene from near the beginning, immediately followed by a scene from near the end. Or vice versa.

Unless you're playing the main part, your scenes may well be attached to a particular location. For example, if your character works in a hospital that the hero visits, that's where your scenes will probably take place. If you're playing the hero's sister, perhaps the hero comes to visit you at your house and that's where your scenes take place. So you will often have all your scenes squeezed into just a few days' filming.

Another consequence of the overriding need to meet the schedule is that there is almost no rehearsal and this can completely wrong-foot an actor used to several weeks of leisurely rehearsal for a theatre production. In another chapter I will go through the actual process of shooting, from walking on to the set to finishing the scene. But for now it will suffice to say that shooting generally involves a few minutes' rehearsal, a relatively long time setting up the shot and then the minimum number of takes required to get what the director wants, before setting up another angle on the same scene and repeating the process. Inexperienced screen actors frequently wonder how they can be expected to do good work without rehearsing properly. The simple answer is that this is exactly what is expected of you. Screen actors must do their preparation beforehand, make maximum use of the few minutes they do get and deliver the goods take after take after take. This is how great movies are made, as well as turkeys, so the process works.

There are numerous other implications of the process of shooting, which I shall explore in the following chapters, but perhaps it's worth summarizing them by saying that everyone involved in filming has two aims, both equally important: *to do good work* and *to meet the schedule*.

Collaboration

Despite the enormous financial and scheduling pressures every production is under, there is also creativity, dedication and artistic sensitivity going on all around you on a film set. Everyone is trying to do his best work and everyone is mutually dependent. The best way to view your role is as a craftsman working in close partnership with other craftsmen on a lovingly and painstakingly constructed artistic collaboration. The worst way is to see yourself is as the pre-eminent artist surrounded by techies whose job is to capture your brilliance for posterity. (Having said that, I'm going to use the word 'technicians' as a collective for the people working in camera and sound).

And just as the other artists on the crew are not merely techies serving you, neither are you merely a puppet. Some inexperienced screen actors fall into the trap of being so eager to please that they obediently do as they are asked, regardless of their own performances to the detriment of both the whole drama and their own careers.

The best film sets are a place of continual low-level negotiation as people strike a balance between these two elements. In the chapter on rehearsal in the section *Doing It*, I'll explore this in more detail.

A word of caution: the technical demands can be a trap for stage actors who pride themselves on their technical proficiency and are feeling vulnerable in the unfamiliar environment of a film set. Not only does it bolster your self-confidence – *'yeah, I can do that'* – but it's a quick route to popularity with key members of the crew who love a technically able and cooperative actor. The audience doesn't know or care whether you effortlessly managed complex manoeuvres that helped the shot. Anything you do that is not fully and vividly connected to your character's inner world of actions and objectives will be exposed by the camera as empty. Put too much attention on the technical and your performance will suffer.

Apart from the other actors in the scene, the person you will work most closely with is the camera operator. If you have more than one or two scenes, make it your business to make friends with him as you can make each other's lives easier. When it works well there are frequent side-conversations between actor and camera operator as they collaborate to produce the best shots. For a full list of other people in the crew, their roles and your involvement with them, see the chapter *'Who's who in the crew'*.

Practice

The more you are on top of the technical demands of filming, the less likely they are to interfere with your performance. Camcorders are dirt cheap and most mobile phones record sufficiently good footage to allow you to practise some of the techniques that follow at home. Even better, hook up with a friend and practise together.

8

UNDERSTANDING THE SHOTS

Understanding a little about the different categories of shots and the important camera terminology can help you know where you are in the process and therefore pace yourself and manage your energy. Though don't get hung up on the detail.

Single versus multi-camera shooting

The overwhelming majority of drama is shot with a single camera because to use more than one involves too many compromises in the lighting (remember, acting is not the only game in town). There may sometimes be a second camera, but this will usually be used to shoot a different sized shot down the same line, that is, from a position adjacent to the first camera.

The exception to this is multi-camera which, as the name suggests, involves several different cameras shooting from different angles. This is only ever used in studio shoots – mostly sitcoms and soap operas – where the photography matters less than the performances. It's best not to mention this to the Director of Photography. He knows, but there's no point in rubbing his nose in it.

Multi-camera is much more like theatre, in that there is effectively a fourth wall, although cameras will often come right into the set. It can easily seduce you into playing to the 'audience' side of the set, where the crew and equipment are, because it *feels* like the audience. And in the case of sitcoms there will sometimes be a live studio audience present. Be wary of falling into this trap. Playing multi-camera may – *may* – involve opening up to this fourth wall, similar to the way you might on stage. But the real audience is still the camera and everything I've written about the perils of 'showing' still applies.

There are a small number of sitcoms, mostly filmed in front of a live studio audience, that implicitly acknowledge the existence of the audience like a surreptitious wink to the television viewer. These are a genre all of their own – shows like *Big Bang Theory* and *My Parents Are Aliens* – and they demand a particular style of playing. Watch someone like David Hyde Pierce playing Niles Crane in the long running series *Frasier* for a masterclass in walking the line between outrageous comedy and naturalism.

What do I need to know about the shots and camera terminology?

I'm not at all convinced that it benefits the screen actor to concern himself too greatly with the specifics of the shot. In any medium there are plenty of obstacles to the actor's goal of living truthfully and, in my opinion, anything that increases these is to be avoided.

There are books on screen acting that go into great detail about framing and composition and the position of the boom and advise actors to make extensive adjustments to their performances accordingly. I argue pretty much the opposite. This is not from any patronizing standpoint of *'don't worry your pretty little head about it'*. And if you really want to know the size of the shot, the closer the boom is, the closer the shot. But what you see in the eyes of an actor who is busy thinking about the frame, rather than experiencing the character's reality, is just that an *actor* who is thinking about the frame rather than a *character* experiencing his reality.

Many of the best screen actors haven't a clue about shot size or composition. Instead they focus on the job of being truthful and spontaneous and, as a side-issue, incorporating what they are asked to do to make the shot work, without worrying about what the shot is. Over the years, more experienced actors may learn to make minor modifications to their performances according to whether the shot is wide or close. But for most, and especially stage actors learning to work on camera, occupying themselves with the difference between a *'dirty single'* and a *'close over-the-shoulder 2-shot'* is not going to help them deliver their best.

Having said that, there are a few basic distinctions that you need to know because it may affect what will be asked of you. And the more at ease you are with the technical demands of filming, the less of your attention they require. This should be your ambition, when it comes to the technical requirements of filming: the ability to execute them with the minimum of attention, so that your focus can be the character's inner world.

In describing the shots, I may even seem to contradict my emphasis on the primacy of the character's reality. But the tension I wrote about earlier, between the actor's reality and the character's reality, can often seem like a contradiction.

9
GLOSSARY OF SHOTS

So here is what you need to know about individual shots:

Master

This is generally the first shot to be done within a scene. It's usually a wide shot of all the action and dialogue and all continuity will usually be matched to this.

Wide/Mid/Close

These terms are fairly self-explanatory. If it's a *'wide'* the camera is seeing most of you, certainly from your knees to the top of your head (Figure 3).

A *'mid-shot'* means anything from your knees or your waist up to the top of your head. Your arms and gestures will be visible in this shot (Figure 4).

The word *'close'* generally means from the top of your head down to about the level of your armpits is in shot. Your shoulders will be visible but your arms probably won't and neither will your hands, unless you lift them into the frame (Figure 5).

Figure 3 Wide shot.

Figure 4 Mid-shot.

Figure 5 Medium Close-Up (MCU).

Figure 6 Prop floating in bottom of frame.

Figure 7 Prop lifted into frame.

If you are handling a prop, you may well be asked to raise it or lower it to avoid the strange effect of a bit of your hand and/or the prop bobbing about in the bottom of the frame (Figures 6 and 7).

Single

A *'single'* means a shot that features just one person. And by *features* I mean the face is visible. If it's a single on the other person, then your face won't be visible, even if a bit of the back of your head is in shot. In the other guy's single, your primary job is to help him do his best work without messing up the composition.

Dirty/Clean

A *'clean'* single means only the subject of the shot is visible in the frame (Figure 8). A *'dirty'* single means some part of the other character – head, shoulder, arm or perhaps hip – visible in the foreground of the frame (Figure 9).

Figure 8 Clean single.

Figure 9 Dirty single.

2 Shot

A '2-shot' features two people, usually side by side (Figure 10).

Figure 10 2-shot.

As well as these basics, it may also be helpful to understand the following commonly used terminology about how the scene will be filmed, so you can understand where you are in the process and manage your energy appropriately:

Tracking shot

The camera will be mounted on a dolly (a fancy trolley) or a small crane or jib arm (a bit like one end of a see-saw) and will move during the take. If it's on a dolly, this will be pushed manually, by the grip, along a specially laid track. On some multi-camera shoots, the cameras may be permanently mounted on large, multipurpose, *go-in-any-direction* platforms called 'peds'. If the camera is on a crane or jib arm it will be controlled either manually or by computer, though this need not concern you. The point is that not only will the camera be moving – either throughout the take or during part of it – but so, probably, will the camera operator, grip, focus puller and often the boom operator. In especially ambitious shots you may be asked to move and hit a mark as well to coincide with the camera movement.

There are three implications of a tracking shot:

1   The shot will take longer to set up and rehearse. Pace yourself and manage your energy.

2   All this movement during the take is distracting and can easily break your concentration.

3   The complexity level goes up. A good take demands precision from everyone involved and if any one of you makes a mistake, even a small one, the shot will probably be no good, so there are likely to be a larger number of takes before you all get it right.

If you deliver a zinging performance only to be told you have to go again because the boom came into shot or the focus was soft, you have to take it in your stride. The other guys are all professionals, doing their best, and they don't complain when they get their bit perfect and you stumble over a line. But it may require deep reserves of concentration to keep delivering your best work through 8, 9 or 10 (or even more) takes.

As the take number rises, everyone feels the pressure to get it right. There may even come a point when the director decides to simplify something and the shot gets rethought, and possibly re-rehearsed, which may include a hiatus for you. Pace yourself and manage your energy.

As well as horizontal movement, there may also be vertical movement. So even when no track is laid, the dolly may *'jib up'* or *'jib down'*. This is usually nothing like as complicated as a tracking shot, although it still has to be timed and the movement itself has the potential to break your concentration.

Coverage

This is the sequence of shots. For example, the most conventional, and quickest, way of covering a two-character dialogue scene – the most common type of scene – is to have the two actors facing each other and film them initially in a wide shot (Figure 11) followed by a CU of each (Figures 12 and 13). So the coverage is three shots in total.

The bigger the budget, and the more time in the schedule, the more complicated the coverage will be. For example, a more complicated scene with four characters might have a master, another wide shot, a 3-shot, a 2-shot and mid-shots and CUs of two of the characters. Probably some or all of these will also involve tracking. So the coverage would be eight shots in total.

While I don't advise you to concern yourself with the detail of the shots, it can be helpful to know: (a) how many shots there will be, so you can pace yourself and (b) when (whether) there will be a CU of you.

You need to deliver your best, most committed work on your CU, so you must keep yourself fresh for this. While you obviously want to be good in every take, performing the scene repeatedly as you work through numerous takes of master shots, 2-shots, mid-shots and other people's CUs can leave you stale by the time you get to your all-important CU. Be generous in giving a performance to help other people in their shots but many of the best actors also hold a little something back for their own.

Set-ups

Each time the camera position changes, it's a new set-up and the lighting and set dressing will usually have to change. This will take anything from a few minutes to an hour (or possibly even longer for a complex shot on a high budget production. For particularly ambitious shots it's not unknown for setting up and rehearsing to take most of the day). This time is an opportunity for the actors to rehearse or relax. Manage your energy and DO NOT LEAVE THE SET WITHOUT CHECKING FIRST WITH THE 3rd AD or THE 1st AD.

Figure 11 Wide master.

Figure 12 Dirty single.

Figure 13 Reverse dirty single.

Reverse

Most scenes are shot with the camera initially facing in one direction only – usually a wide and some closer shots. At some point in the coverage the camera will be turned around to face in the other direction – the 'reverses' (see Figure 13). This means a long hiatus as all the equipment and upwards of 30 people behind the camera have to be moved to the other side of the set.

Slate

A new shot. Even if the camera position and/or the lighting has not changed, if the parameters of the frame have changed – perhaps the shot is looser or tighter or the focus has changed – it's a new slate. This does not need to concern you unless it's a change from a wide shot to a close shot and you are sufficiently experienced to want to make a slight adjustment in scale to your performance. With a new slate, as opposed to a new set-up, it should only take a few minutes before the camera is ready to roll for the next take.

Working with technophile/ geek actors

Having said that actors do not need to concern themselves too much with the shot, there are a few actors who relish the technical challenges and like to know the detail. They may well be listening carefully during the discussion of the coverage and plan their performance according to it. Do not be put off by this. It does not make them superior actors to you. Neither does it make them inferior. There are many approaches to the relationship between the technical and the emotional and your task is to find what works for *you*.

I once directed a scene between two actors who could not have been more different in the way they approached the work. One was highly technical and stepped out of character the moment I said *'cut'*, usually with a quip or a comment on what had happened during the take. He would then ask questions or offer opinions about the filming process.

The other actor was intensely personal, uninterested in anything technical (though perfectly capable of delivering what was needed) and remained in character throughout the scene, disappearing off into corners between set-ups to sustain herself. Both were rising stars and delivered superb performances. Each had their own way of working and both have gone on to have highly successful careers. Whether the second actor was bothered by the radically different approach of the first (which bordered on the disrespectful) I never discovered.

If the technophile sounds like you and you enjoy acquiring your own technical mastery, then just let me repeat my warning that you focus too much on the technical at your peril. Make damn sure that during the take the overwhelming majority of your attention is on living truthfully in the imaginary circumstances.

The next section of the book is in two parts. The first deals with the things you'll be asked to do by heads of department within the crew to assist them in their work, for example, camera, sound, etc. The second *'Working the camera'* describes techniques you can use to make your performance work better on camera.

10
HITTING MARKS

Movements within the scene are carefully plotted and you will
frequently be required to stop on a precise mark indicated by
coloured tape on the floor. You must be able to do this without
needing to look down to find your mark. Most actors do this by
using peripheral vision, counting the number of places or lining up
peripheral objects.

Marks

In searching constantly for the perfect shot composition, the operator
will ask you to do certain things to place you where he wants you in the
frame or to make sure you are in focus. In particular, he will need you to
stand in certain places for parts of the scene. These are your *'marks'*,
usually T-shapes of brightly coloured tape on the floor.

You will be expected to hit your marks on demand. Occasionally
the reason may be evident to you – this is something that comes with
experience and the operator will usually be happy to explain if you really
want to know – but more often than not you won't know specifically
why you're being asked to hit the mark, you just need to do it.

In Figures 14–17 you'll see a couple of examples of the difference it
can make to the composition.

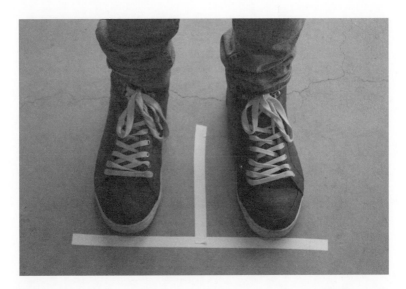

Figure 14 On mark.

Figure 15 Balanced composition.

Figure 16 Off mark.

Figure 17 Composition no good.

Focus

The *'depth of field'* is the amount of space that is in focus. By varying the lens and the amount of light, the Director of Photography (DoP) can alter the depth of field and isolate an object in the frame. For example, in Figure 15 the actor is lifted out of the background by being in focus – *'sharp'* – where both the foreground actor and the background are out of focus or *'soft'*. Miss your mark – too far forward or back – and you may be soft in which case the take is no good.

What the DoP would very often like to do is make the depth of field very shallow, a matter of inches, but he can only do this if the actor can reliably hit his mark precisely. He will quickly figure out which actors are capable of this and, of course, he and the director will love those they can rely on. For those who only ever hit their marks approximately, he will need to go for a wider depth of field, which compromises the shot.

Putting down marks

The position of marks will be set to the particular shot and many will not need a mark at all, either because rough positioning will suffice or because the floor is visible so any mark would show up in the frame.

If a mark is needed, you will be asked to walk through the shot as part of setting up, stopping and starting, while the camera assistant puts down the marks. The camera operator may adjust these later in the process as he tries to get the composition perfect.

While you are expected to deliver what's asked in terms of movement and positioning, if it involves something that feels plain wrong, in terms of emotion and motivation, it's worth asking if the positioning can be adjusted to accommodate what works for you. Everybody wants you to deliver a fantastic performance and a sensitive camera operator or director will not usually want you to be doing something that will get in the way of this. This is the kind of negotiation I referred to earlier. And just as with every other member of the team, the director is much more likely to listen to you, whether it's a problem with a mark or a request to do another take, if he experiences you most of the time as reliable and helpful.

How to hit your marks

There are three main techniques that actors use to hit their marks.

1 Peripheral vision

The tape used for marks is brightly coloured to help you see it with your peripheral vision (Figure 18). The challenge of using your peripheral vision is that as you get near the mark, it disappears from your field of view, so it requires good spatial coordination to judge where it is once you can no longer see it (Figure 19).

What absolutely does not work is glancing down to locate your mark. You cannot do this without the audience noticing. You may think you can, but you can't. And as the editor and director put the cut together, they will watch you do so again and again and probably have to find a way of cutting round it. That's not to say that some actors don't get quite clever at emotionally motivating a reason for their character to look down, just at the precise moment the actor needs to see where the mark is. This is not something I'd particularly recommend, although you can often get away with it once or twice during a shoot before the director starts to think of you as *'that actor who always looks down to find his mark'*.

If you're colour-blind, make sure you let the camera assistant know early in the shoot and he will use whatever colour tape is most visible to you. Similarly, even if you're not colour-blind, if you find one colour easier to see than others, let him know. He'll be happy to help you because doing so will help make the shot better.

2 Counting paces

Knowing exactly how many paces there are from your start point to your mark will enable you to hit it fairly accurately, as long as you're reasonably well coordinated and your stride length is reliably the same. You'll need a start mark so you always begin the exact number of paces from your end mark. To fix this, stand on your mark, turn around and walk forwards towards your start point until you are

Figure 18 Actor's point of view (POV): Mark on floor in foreground.

Figure 19 Actor's POV: Mark no longer visible as you approach it.

clear of the frame – work with the operator and camera assistant to establish this.

Aim for as few paces as possible because you're less likely to over or under-shoot your mark. But do make sure they're regular paces. By having to remember to take larger or smaller steps you just make things harder for yourself.

If you have dialogue as you're walking and have to finish it just as you hit your mark, *back-time* it. This means you start on your end mark and walk (forwards) towards your start point, running the lines normally until you reach the place in the dialogue where you must hit your mark. Wherever you are is your starting point, so ask the camera assistant to mark it for you.

If your mark is not an exact number of paces from your required starting point, you have to make a choice between walking normally and adding a quarter/half/three quarters pace at the end or taking slightly larger (or smaller) strides.

As you get more confident/experienced it's occasionally worth checking with the camera operator if the positioning of the mark is critical or whether it can be adjusted to make an even number of paces for you. The answer may be 'no', but not always.

3 Lining up objects

This less well-known technique only works on a set or location with props or fixtures. When you stand on your mark, look to see if two objects line up perfectly in your peripheral vision. Or perhaps objects can be moved so they line up? In either case you simply walk forwards until you reach the point where they are in line with each other and you are now on your mark. For example, in Figures 20–22 there are a tree and a drainpipe to the right of the actor. As the point of view approaches the actor, the drainpipe gets closer to the tree until it disappears behind it.

Different techniques suit different actors and most use a combination according to the situation and their own preference. If you're having any problem, there is an additional resource available to you: the sausage.

Figure 20 Actor's POV: Tree and drainpipe separated.

Figure 21 Actor's POV: Tree and drainpipe closer.

Figure 22 Actor's POV: Drainpipe obscured behind tree. You've hit your mark!

The soft bag

The soft bag, commonly known in the United Kingdom as a *'sausage'*, is a canvas tube about the same size as a large courgette, that can be taped to the floor as your mark. When you reach it, you can feel it with your foot, making it much easier to hit your mark with accuracy.

For some reason, many actors let their pride get in the way of asking for one of these, preferring instead to struggle on, trying (and often failing) to hit their mark using one of the other techniques. This is really irritating for a director who has to use up precious time doing repeated takes because an actor is too proud to accept help. Everybody understands how difficult it is to hit a mark accurately and wants to help. So if you're offered a sausage, I'd advise you to accept. It doesn't mean you've failed, it simply means the camera crew knows how hard your task is. And if you need one, ask for one. Not only will no one think less of you, they will regard it as a sign of your professionalism that you ask for what you need to get the job done. (And by the way, everyone on set has got over the joke of it being called a sausage, so while it may still amuse you – and no reason why it shouldn't – you won't get laughed at for calling it this).

Similarly, if you're using the technique of lining up objects and someone off-camera is obscuring your view, ask him (politely) to move. He will, of course, be completely unaware of what you're doing and only too happy to move if it will help you make the shot work.

The real challenge

Hitting your mark is a necessary part of making the short work. But it's not an end in itself for you. The challenge for an actor is to make the shot work without losing his emotional commitment to the scene. Because the camera sees so closely, if your attention is on hitting your mark, this is what the audience will see in your eyes. Or at the very least it will register a detachment, a tiny moment of emotional vacancy. As I mentioned in the chapter on listening, the editor and director will trawl through your performance in the cutting room, selecting the richest and most vividly lived moments and rejecting any lapse in concentration.

So, the more adept you become at hitting your mark, whichever technique you use, the less of your attention it requires.

Practice

Block out a scene that sees you moving. Use coloured tape (electrical tape from a hardware store) to give yourself marks and practise the three techniques to make the moves, while continuing to focus on your emotional intention. Ideally, record yourself doing this, making sure you set up a frame that sees you come in to close up as you hit the mark as this is what will reveal whether you're still in the scene or have a glazed look in your eyes as you search for your mark.

11
OVERLAPS

Overlaps are one of the most technically demanding aspects of screen acting. When asked to do a take with *'no overlaps'*, you must make sure there is a tiny gap between your dialogue and that of the other actors, even if, in story terms, you interrupt each other.

Why overlaps matter

You will occasionally hear the call from the sound recordist or 1st AD *'no overlaps'*. The best way to explain this is using an example:

A

All you ever do is. . .

B

You don't know what you're talking about!

The most obvious way of playing this exchange is with B interrupting A (although it could be that A simply peters out), in which case there will be a brief moment when both are talking at the same time. This is an overlap and is what you may be asked to avoid.

A: ━━━━━━━━━━

B: ━━━━━━━━━━

The reason this matters is that if the exchange is shot as a master and close-ups (CU) of each character, the editor may end up with double sound as he cuts from CU to CU.

Let's say that, as rehearsed and shot in the master, B interrupts A just as A begins to say *'is . . .'*. When the wide shot is used both voices can be heard overlapping, which matches the lip movement there's no problem.

But the microphones that pick up the clearest sound are unidirectional, that is, they record only in the direction they are pointed. So on A's CU the sound of his dialogue will be perfect but B's dialogue will be off-mic, that is, indistinct. So if B's words *'You don't know . . .'* overlap with A's words *'. . . do is . . .'* there's a mixture of on-mic and off-mic sound which cannot be separated. And when the editor then adds in the sound from B's CU of B's dialogue (on-mic) it also has on it the sound of A's dialogue (off-mic) overlapping. So at the moment of overlap in the CUs there will simultaneously be two versions of A saying *'. . . do is . . .'* and two versions of B saying *'You don't know . . .'*.

What the editor needs is an air gap, that is, a microsecond of silence between A finishing speaking and B starting to speak so he can cut from A's clean dialogue (from A's CU) to B's clean dialogue (from B's CU). He will then slip B's CU forward until the two lines of dialogue overlap in the edit and B interrupts A, as he does in the wide shot.

If you're having trouble following this explanation – and I don't blame you, it is complicated – don't worry. The thing you need to know is that when you're told *'no overlaps'* you and the other actors must leave this air gap between any lines of dialogue. So if you interrupt another character on the wide shot, you must let him stop talking before coming in with your line. And if you are interrupted by another character, you need to peter out **as though you have been interrupted**, even though he won't actually interrupt you. Instead, a split second after you've stopped talking, the other actor will come in with his line.

In theory, this is fairly straightforward. But in practice it's quite technically demanding and harder than it sounds. The principal difficulty comes in maintaining the energy and momentum of interrupting and being interrupted. Because when we interrupt others we tend to raise the volume slightly and speak a tiny bit faster in order to break through. Then, when the other person has stopped talking, effectively allowing us the floor, we slow down slightly and probably lower the volume fractionally.

Similarly when someone tries to interrupt us, we will often increase the volume and pace in order to resist before taking the decision to stop talking. All this goes on subconsciously but if these changes are missing, the audience will feel something is wrong, even if they don't know *what* is wrong.

Just as in the theatre, you should always know what you are going to say and have the rest of your sentence ready to speak in case the other character does not interrupt you. Perhaps in the example above A was going to say *'. . . complain.'* Explicitly agree with your partner how it will work, for example, that you'll stop after the 's' of *'. . . is . . .'* or the 'm' of *'complain'* and grab any opportunity you get to rehearse this interruption without overlaps.

You'll find that stopping yourself as though you've been interrupted is much easier to sell on a plosive at the beginning of the word. A plosive is a consonant that involves a little burst of energy as the lips or teeth separate, like a mini explosion in the mouth, and the most useful are those that are obvious when begun but not actually voiced, for example, *'b', 'm', 'n', 'p'* or *'t'*, because they allow you to start to formulate the next word with your lips and be visibly stopped by the other person's interruption. For example, if you're playing A, it's easier to stop yourself as you begin to formulate the 'p' of *'. . . complain'* than the 'i' of *'. . . is . . .'* because the latter is open-ended in the mouth.

And, if you're playing B, you need to know exactly where A is going to stop so you can come in with your line a split second after A has stopped, so the momentum of the scene is not derailed.

It's worth pointing out that this doesn't only apply to dialogue where a line is written as incomplete by the writer. If, in the playing of any scene, one character interrupts the other or there is a marginal overlap simply because of the energy of the exchange, you may be similarly asked not to do overlaps. However, you will generally only be asked to avoid them for CUs because the sound on wide shots is rarely used and, even if it is, both mouths are in vision so the problem doesn't exist. Eventually, as you get more experienced on screen, you will start to recognize when you're going to be asked to avoid overlaps and perhaps even anticipate it.

12
CONTINUITY

Continuity is an indispensible professional skill. You won't get any credit for doing it right, but you will frustrate the director in the edit if you have made mistakes. Large movements must be reproduced with exact timing, smaller movements are less critical. Being aware of the external or internal impulse that caused the action is the surest way to get it right.

Why continuity matters

You're probably already aware that the need for continuity exists, that is, you have to do the same thing in every take. But there is often some confusion among stage actors over quite how precise this has to be. In a nutshell, it's the larger physical actions – your posture, gesture and movements – that must match. Smaller movements, for example, nodding your head, eye movements, sighing, changes in facial expression, etc. generally don't matter. If you drum your fingers on a table for part of a scene, you must drum your fingers in the same part of the scene on every take. The precise pattern of finger movement is not important.

It's helpful to understand a little about why continuity is so significant. The edit is assembled from clips lasting only a few seconds from numerous different takes. This is not only a question of changing the camera angle; different moments from different takes of the same slate will be used. For example, the director may like the way you said your second line in take 2 of the close-up (CU), but prefer take 4 for your third line.

It's fairly obvious that if you are holding a cup in your right hand in one take and your left hand in another, the audience is likely to notice. We've all seen enough out-take shows in which props jump around the scene to understand this. But what you never get to see in the finished work is the degree to which continuity errors – by actors or in the set dressing – limit the director's choices when editing.

Actors tend to fall into three camps when it comes to continuity: flawless, pretty good but with the occasional mistake and wretched. Obviously directors love the actors whose continuity is flawless (as long as it's not at the expense of their performance) and think nothing too terrible of the majority who make the occasional mistake. But there is a special place in hell reserved for actors whose continuity is all over the place. The tail wags the dog as the edit becomes dominated by trying to piece together something workable rather than letting the story and the drama drive the decision-making.

Let's say a director has filmed a scene with two characters, A and B, talking. He opens the scene on a wide shot. He then decides to cut to a single of A. But he finds that A had his arms crossed in the single, unlike in the wide shot, so can't cut until A uncrosses his arms.

After a few seconds A does so and his position matches the wide. But by now, B has looked down in A's dirty single, which can be seen in the foreground and which contradicts the wide shot. So the director still can't cut.

He waits for B to look up again in A's single or to look down in the wide shot. By the point in the scene when B does so in the wide, A has leant forward and gestured with his hands. But he didn't do this in the single, so the director *still* can't cut.

And by the time A's posture in the single matches the wide shot again, B has done something else that contradicts the wide shot.

So the entire scene ends up being played on the wide. Aaaaaargh!

Some of these movements were as rehearsed and they all derived from the actors being spontaneous and truthful, playing their actions and pursuing their objectives. Both actors were fully aware of the need for continuity and, if asked, would have told you they had performed the same actions in the same place. Even the clear mistakes felt right during the take. But unfortunately, despite delivering compelling performances, they massively reduced the director's options for cutting.

It's worth remembering that a large part of the final impression you create on a director is formed by the weeks or months he has spent in a cutting room, going over and over your performance in the edit. Of course this is quite likely to be the time when an in-demand director is beginning to think about the casting of his next project. (It's true that in the example above, the script supervisor, whose job it is to monitor continuity, would also be pretty unlikely to get hired again by that director. But that's cold comfort.)

Movement drives the cut

You can sometimes get away with inconsistent continuity as long as there's no movement to draw attention to it. But movement has another very important part to play in editing because it is often used to motivate the cut. Just as everything in an actor's performance needs to be motivated, so too does every editing decision. Each time the shot changes, it fractionally disrupts the viewer's engagement. In a well-edited piece each cut offers the audience a change of view that they want to see. For example, a character in a CU hears somebody coming into the room and turns his head to see who it is. The audience wants to see who it is and the character's head-turn will 'throw' the cut to a shot of the door.

A frustrated lover in a wide shot pauses between thoughts and looks away briefly before turning back and launching into an accusation against his partner. The look-away is emotionally prompted by uncertainty over whether to make the accusation and the mustering of courage. The turn-back is the moment of decision and we, the audience, want to look closer at this moment to see the intensity of feeling so the cut to a CU is motivated. As we'll explore in Chapter 16 'Playing the Camera' (which explains *the Doughnut*) skilled actors may achieve the same thing merely by breaking eye contact rather than turning the whole head, but the principle is the same: eye movement can be used by the editor to motivate the cut in just the same way.

How to manage your continuity

Your initial posture is relatively easy to identify and to return to at the start of each take. It's likely that your training and experience on stage has sufficiently developed your physical awareness that you will either remember your posture without prompting or can take in your stride a reminder from the script supervisor. My advice is to start each scene from the same emotional standpoint, following on from whatever backstory you have created for the character, in particular relating to what has just happened before the scene begins.

What's more difficult is precisely reproducing movements within the scene.

To some degree, muscle memory can help you. And rehearsing the movement and dialogue together in small, private moments of rehearsal, whenever you are not needed elsewhere, can help train your body to do it automatically. But you must also develop the habit of being conscious about your movements. Allow yourself to rehearse freely with the director and other actors, then monitor your movements as the scene is shown to the crew. Showing is about communicating to the crew what will happen, not giving a definitive performance of massive emotional intensity.

By far the hardest way of managing your continuity is to remember it by rote. The script supervisor can tell you when you did certain things or which hand was holding which object, but this is merely a physical description and if you are having to use your memory actively, it's likely that this will show in your eyes. It never ceases to amaze me how, in the cutting room, you can actually see thoughts change on an actor's face. This includes when they lose their concentration or step out of the character's reality to deal with something technical. In these moments the inner monologue is visibly the actor's, not the character's. And these are not moments you want to put in front of an audience.

So rather than relying on your memory and hoping to hide what you're actually focusing on, far better to remember it through the character's inner monologue.

Every physical action is a response to a stimulus, either internal or external. Sometimes in a scene your character will move in response to an external stimulus. This might be, for example, another character threatening you and causing you to step back. If the other actor threatens you at a different place in the script, you will step back in response at a different, and wrong, place. So your continuity is dependent on his continuity and it may need some explicit discussion to make this consistent and reliable.

The external stimulus may also be something inanimate, such as a car passing or a doorbell. If it's something visual within the frame, you can rely on an Assistant Director (AD) or one in the art department to give you the cue in the right place. But if it's an audio cue, these usually don't happen at all on set because the sound recordist will want to record the synch (i.e. live) sound as cleanly as possible and they'll add the sound effect in post-production. Consequently you have to react to a non-existent sound. If you find this difficult it's perfectly acceptable to ask for an AD to mark the moment of the cue to give you something to react to. Don't be shy – just ask.

But most of your continuity will be dictated by your response to internal stimuli, that is, your own thoughts and feelings. Managing the inner monologue is by far the best way to deliver continuity.

Imagine you are playing my lover and we have the following exchange.

                          YOU
          You've slept with her, haven't you?

                          ME
          No, of course I haven't.

In fact you're right: I got drunk and gave in to temptation. Consider the three following physical responses I might make:

1 I look down briefly then look up again to deliver my line.

2 I look away to the side briefly before looking back to deliver my line.

3 I look away to the side and avoid looking at you while delivering my line

Now let's identify the inner monologue that might drive them and the subtext of my response.

1. I look down briefly then look up again to deliver my line.

Inner monologue: *'How did she find out? I bitterly regret it but that's not going to pacify her. Deny it.'*

Dominant emotion: guilt

Subtext of the delivery: *'Please believe me, I would never do that.'*

2. I look away to the side briefly before looking back to deliver my line.

Inner monologue: *'Okay, so she suspects. I have nothing to feel guilty about – she deserved it for ignoring me – but I don't want the hassle of having an argument about it. Deny it.'*

Dominant emotions: irritation and self-righteousness

Subtext of the delivery: *'Don't be so stupid, of course I haven't. Why on earth are you accusing me of that?'*

3. I look away to the side and avoid looking at you while delivering my line.

Inner monologue: *'Oh God. If I admit it she'll leave me. I'll pretend I've got nothing to feel guilty about and that I'm not worried. But I mustn't look at her or she'll know.'*

Dominant emotion: fear

Subtext of the delivery: *'What an extraordinary accusation! How could you even think such a thing?'*

Whichever of the three I am playing, as long as I return to the same emotional point at the start of each take, then my inner monologue should be roughly the same, and that will give rise to the same physical continuity.

Of course, these are only three from a vast number of possible emotional and physical responses, all of which lead to the same scripted response *'no, of course I haven't'*. And if the backstory is not that specific for example, whether you're right, whether it's the first time, whether you've been unfaithful yourself, etc. then this increases my possibilities still further.

I don't suggest plotting out a particular response beforehand in order to keep the continuity. If I do this, I'm very likely to lose my sense of spontaneity and emotional connection to you and Stanislavski's unbroken line will be broken.

When it comes to continuity there's a crucial difference between the macro and micro. The macro – the overall thrust of the scene and the larger movements and actions – demands continuity. And yet, if I'm truly listening, and therefore willing to let you change me, what I feel will also be dependent on what I perceive in you. So the micro – the minutiae of feeling and impulse and listening and reaction – must be alive and fresh and present and probably different on each and every take.

It's almost impossible to define exactly where the macro stops and the micro begins. But to return to Sir Ben Kingsley's tennis metaphor, the continuity is the white lines down the side of the court: it's the actor's job to hit the ball across the net and into the court and there are people who will call it out if you don't.

If you are absolutely clear on your personal history, your relationship with the other characters and your emotional state at the beginning of the scene, and if you can reliably find the emotional response that drives the physical response and add in a bit of muscle memory, your continuity will be consistent.

A lot of this will be familiar, in one form or another, from your work on stage where you need to connect dialogue with movement in a similar way. Most stage actors do this intuitively. But there is scope in the theatre to reinvent the detail of the blocking every night, as long as you observe the broader parameters. Whereas on screen, every take must reproduce the same physicality and, to make it that little bit harder, if doing so is effortful, this will be instantly visible.

Emotional continuity

In addition to physical continuity, there also needs to be some emotional continuity between takes.

When you really start exploring a scene, it's often astonishing how wildly different interpretations are viable. Many, many scenes can be made to work with a through line of anger or tenderness or apology or embarrassment or defiance. But trying to edit together a strongly angry interpretation by an actor in one take with a strongly apologetic interpretation in another take is an almost impossible task. (And remember, the director is very likely to be selecting different moments from different takes, rather than using one single take of your performance.) So, broadly speaking, there needs to be a continuity of through-line between takes.

The best actors make very efficient use of the limited rehearsal time to explore the potential of various interpretations and feel their way towards something compelling and truthful with their fellow performers. Even as the scene is being shown to the crew, they are emotionally experimenting, while committing themselves to the physical actions around which the technicians will build their work. This exploration can even continue as the shot is being set up, with moments of rehearsal grabbed wherever possible. But once the first take is in the can (and the director or 1st AD will sometimes call *'let's match to that'*, by which he means everything that follows should be consistent with that take), they repeat the main thrust of the interpretation, while still spontaneously creating the emotional nuances moment-by-moment in response to their own inner impulses and whatever comes at them externally.

What does not work is to reproduce your performance mechanically take after take. If you do, your continuity may be wonderful but your acting will probably suck. Rather, there is a balance to be struck between, on the one hand, the freedom and spontaneity that makes for compelling, truthful performance and, on the other, the discipline and professionalism that continuity demands.

Practice

Get used to playing scenes with a conscious awareness of the impulses that create your movements. Practise playing a scene – ideally with a partner but alone if necessary – and, immediately afterwards, run through the scene again, clocking what you did physically and the impulse that created the moment.

13

POSITIONING YOURSELF FOR THE CAMERA

When being filmed in a 'dirty single' try to keep a consistent distance between the head of the other actor and the camera, to help the composition. Scenes are often shot from opposing angles and you can frequently help the coverage by favouring one direction or the other.

Opposing singles

The most common way of filming two characters facing each other is in opposing singles. The director will often want to bring your eyeline close to the camera so the audience can see into your eyes (Figures 23 and 24). This will bring all sorts of other things directly into your field of vision behind the other actor, like the camera team and the boom operator. This has the potential to break your concentration and even the most fleeting lapses will register on camera.

Figure 23 Eyeline away from camera.

Figure 24 Eyeline close to camera.

If the shot is a dirty single, the distance between the head of the other actor and the camera becomes significant in terms of composition. You can inadvertently make the shot unusable by slight shifts of your weight, either half-masking yourself behind the other actor's head or forcing the camera operator to choose between letting you go out of the frame or losing the back of the other actor's head from the foreground.

So you should aim to keep a slight distance between the head of the other actor and the camera (Figure 25). Doing this will maintain the operator's composition (Figure 26).

Figure 25 Actor's POV: Good distance between partner's head and the camera.

Figure 26 Resulting shot: Balanced composition.

When the other actor's head and the camera come too close to each other (Figure 27) the result will be 'stacked' composition (Figure 28).

Figure 27 Actor's POV: Partner's head and camera too close.

Figure 28 Resulting shot: Stacked composition.

And if there's too much distance between your partner's head and the camera (Figure 29) you will be too separated in the frame (Figure 30).

Figure 29 Actor's POV: Too much distance between partner's head and camera.

Figure 30 Resulting shot: Composition too loose.

Key to this is often planting yourself squarely on your feet, especially when hitting a mark. If your balance is off and your weight is on one foot or the other, you're much more likely to make a slight shift that is enough to spoil the composition.

Finding the camera

A more advanced technique for helping the composition is what's known as *'finding the camera'*. This is nothing more complicated than understanding that if you can't see the camera, the camera can't see you.

If the camera is obscured by, or almost overlapping with, the head of the actor you're opposite (Figure 27) or some other foreground object then the shot will either be unusable or, at best, compromised (Figure 28). This will probably be because someone (you, your partner, the grip) – has missed his mark.

So if you realize the camera is hidden from you behind another actor or object, simply shift your weight until it appears in your peripheral vision with a little bit of space between (Figure 25). You will instantly become the camera team and director's favourite actor.

I should stress that (a) this is always done with peripheral vision, *never* by looking at the camera directly, and (b) I would discourage you from even thinking about this unless you are able to do so without cost to your performance. As I mentioned before, it's easy for technically adept actors to fall into the trap of helping everybody else do their jobs but sabotaging their own performance in the process. Your job, first and foremost, is to be brilliant when the director says *'action'* and so the character's reality must dominate your inner world. Most directors would prefer a slightly lesser composition and a brilliant performance from you than have a perfect composition and a weak performance.

On occasion you may even be explicitly asked to find the camera in the shot if, for example, they can't put down a mark because it would be visible in the frame. Though they'll tend not to ask this of you unless their sense is that you can cope with it.

Reverses

If you find yourself with your back to the camera at the start of the coverage, it's very likely that there will be a reverse, that is, a shot facing the other way, to capture your performance. Certainly in a dialogue between two characters who are facing each other, there will usually be a single on one character, then a reverse on the other. So there is no need to find reasons to turn yourself towards the camera.

If during the scene, however, the blocking involves you turning towards or away from the camera, make sure you turn **fully** towards or away from it, especially if you have dialogue. There will almost certainly be a reverse (ask the camera operator) and significant moments – including reactions – have much less impact in profile. And try to avoid delivering any dialogue *whilst turning* because this makes it hard both for the boom operator to catch it and the audience to follow it. Either speak the line and then turn. Or turn and then speak the line. In essence you're aiming to deliver all moments of performance towards one camera position or its reverse.

Standing up and sitting down

When you stand up (or sit down) you create a difficult move for the camera operator, who is trying to keep you in the frame in a perfect composition. Sudden, quick movements make it almost impossible for him to do this. So you need to work with him, firstly by letting him know when in the dialogue you will get up (or sit). And secondly by completing the action more slowly than you might in real life. By slowing down the movement you make it much, much easier to contain you in the frame.

14
THE VOICE

There's no need to project your voice and doing so will instantly strike a false note. Beware mumbling. It's not the same thing as being naturalistic and can be intensely frustrating for directors and the audience.

Projection

In writing about the need to avoid showing I've focused on the visual, but the same is true for your voice on screen. In fact, to some extent, it's even more true for the voice which carries the truth. There's a good reason why lie-detectors work by analysing vocal patterns. Truth is far, far harder to fake in the voice than on the face. Consequently, radio is one of the most difficult media to work in. Standing in front of a microphone, clutching a script because there's insufficient time to learn it, the imaginative leap to a fictional world is a huge one and partly explains why radio drama doesn't always meet its ambitions.

On screen the audience is privileged to be able to hear everything that happens without any need on your part to project. This lack of projection can be another difficult adjustment for experienced stage actors, particularly those accustomed to performing in large theatres. Very occasionally you might be asked by the boom operator to raise your volume slightly because of some external factor like a noisy road nearby. But otherwise you can, and must, simply speak truthfully, as you would when communicating with the other characters in the imaginary circumstances, ignoring everything else around you. And this does mean communicating in the *imaginary*, not the actual, circumstances. If the scene is set in a library you can really whisper. If it's set by the side of a motorway you may need to shout, even if you're actually shooting in a quiet backstreet.

A good example of the difference between actual and imaginary circumstances, and a common problem when shooting, is scenes set in nightclubs. The sound of the music will always be added later in post-production because it's essential for the sound recordist to get the dialogue clean so it can all be edited with maximum control. But the characters have to shout because that's what we do when there's lots of ambient noise. What happens is that the production will play a burst of loud music immediately before the take so the actors can adjust their volume levels. In most cases, for the first ten seconds after *'action',* the actors do indeed shout but gradually, as the scene continues, levels slowly drop until, by the end of the scene, they're just talking normally. You may have thought you played the scene brilliantly, full of emotional connection and truth. But the director will ask you to go again because the volume level faded and he can't use your wonderful performance.

Mumbling

There's also an important distinction between volume and clarity. We're perfectly capable of failing to understand speech delivered at an adequate volume because of poor diction. Be very wary of confusing mumbling with authenticity.

Writers labour to craft lines of dialogue that are then crawled over by script editors, producers and directors until every single word has been argued over and justified. For an audience, failing to understand what a character just said because of bad diction is usually an intensely frustrating experience.

Brando may have pioneered a style of naturalism that sometimes involved mumbling, but if you watch him in *On the Waterfront*, it's a significant part of his characterization that Terry Molloy is an inarticulate man for whom words are a challenge. When he talks to Edie, he mumbles because he's smitten with her and the words are not really what the scene is about. But when he famously tells his brother that he *'coulda been a contender, instead of a bum'* we hear it all. Watch him in *Julius Caesar* and every word of Shakespeare's poetry is clear.

Similarly, the *mumblecore* indie film movement centres on confused teenagers and characters in their early twenties whose inarticulacy and uncertainty manifests itself in their speech. We don't always hear their words clearly because their thoughts are not clear and they struggle to express themselves. This is very different to actors failing to articulate lines of dialogue that have been toiled over. Added to which mumblecore directors are deliberately obliging the audience to struggle to understand what's going on for the characters, to underscore what's **not** being said.

15
FACIAL AWARENESS

> Your face, and especially your eyes and mouth, is the most significant part of your instrument on screen and you must develop a deep awareness of what is happening on it, much as you are probably already aware of what's happening in your body.

Facial awareness

When I was in my first significant school play, I had the part of an army general who had to deliver an angry speech. At one rehearsal I thought I was making a pretty good job of it, but the teacher/director stopped me mid-flow and told me that I looked apologetic. He pointed to my foot, which was twisting as I spoke. As a 16-year-old schoolboy, I had no awareness of what was happening in my body unless I specifically directed my attention to it. Three years of voice and movement classes at drama school helped me to cultivate an actor's awareness and your own training and experience should have helped you develop your instrument in the same way.

For the screen, you need a similarly advanced awareness of what is happening on your face because the audience will be thin-slicing from how your inner thoughts and emotions are expressed on it.

Eye movement

We read a lot into where people look and when. Insecurity and broader uncertainty reveal themselves through nervous, darting glances. The focus of our concerns is revealed by our eye movement and the audience understands much about your inner monologue from the timing and direction of your eye movement: when you look from one character to another, when you look up, when you look down, when you turn away, and so on. For a great example of this, look at the scene in *Before Sunrise* when Ethan Hawke and Julie Delpy's characters listen to a record in a listening booth. Neither speaks for about 20 seconds but it couldn't be clearer that he's considering kissing her and she knows it. Second by second you see his indecision and her response to this.

Blinking

In his book *Acting in Film*, Michael Caine advises male actors not to blink on screen if they want to be strong. And it's certainly true that blinking conveys a certain softness. Think how effectively Hugh Grant uses lots of rapid blinking and how it makes him seem unthreatening and charming. In *Elizabeth: The Golden Age* Clive Owen, as Sir Walter Raleigh, blinks only a handful of times in the entire film, including steadfastly not blinking in some quite long takes. It's part of what makes him seem inviolable. Though I'd advise you against attempting something similar unless you have put in some serious practice at *not* blinking. Film lights make most actors more prone to blinking, especially contact lens wearers, and an actor whose eyes are watering will struggle to resist an inner monologue that is entirely about the need to blink. (You may already know the actors' trick of looking into a light and not blinking to provoke tears. It works, but unless you can bring about the accompanying emotion this will seem exactly as empty as it is).

But your blinking is more than a simple indicator of your tough-guy status. It is another powerful gauge of what's going on internally and is therefore an essential part of your self-expression. When we're stressed or surprised, we may blink more rapidly. At other times when we're surprised – a different type of surprise perhaps, shock or fear – we may stop blinking entirely. Anger, compassion, confusion, disappointment, sympathy and many other emotional responses to what's happening internally and externally will all affect our blinking and will therefore be read by the audience.

Around the eyes

The muscles around your eye sockets are enormously expressive and every tiny movement, every slight tensing or relaxing, communicates your inner state.

Eye contact

Intimacy happens through eye contact. You've probably had the experience of catching a stranger's eye on a train or a bus. Usually you look away quickly. In Western culture once you look into someone's eyes for more than about 2 ½ seconds, it takes you into the territory of intimacy. You are looking fully into another person's world and there is real connection. With strangers this often means sexual connection – flirting – or hostility. With friends we seek sympathy and concord, though sometimes we get the opposite.

We also frequently use eye contact to establish dominance and submission. You probably know how hard it is it to maintain eye contact with someone who intimidates you and you may have known that someone else was intimidated by you because they couldn't hold your eye.

All of this is read by the screen audience. The director and editor decide when to show eye contact through the cut, but they are only working with the material you give them.

The mouth and the jaw

After the eyes, the next most expressive part of the face is the mouth. We express a lot of emotion in the shape and movement of our mouths and therefore audiences watch them closely, even if they don't necessarily know they're doing so.

There are many hundreds of movements our mouths make, involving lips, teeth, tongue and jawbone. Like your eyes, the muscles around your mouth are extremely complex and often directly express your feelings. Jut your lower jaw forward only slightly and it suggests something about how you feel. Do the same with your mouth closed and it means something else. Purse your lips and it's different. Draw back the corners of your mouth and the meaning changes again. And so on, endless variation, endlessly expressive.

Swallowing

Like blinking, swallowing frequently happens involuntarily in response to emotion and in ways that are far more subtle than the cartoon *'gulp'* at something alarming. At times the audience will read meaning about your emotional state into your swallowing.

Using this awareness

Just as the stage actor who plans or choreographs what to do with his hands risks losing the connection with spontaneity, so the screen actor who is too deliberate with his eyes and mouth will probably do the same. But your face is the single most expressive part of your instrument and the audience will register and interpret every tiny change in your expression.

In the same way you have developed an awareness, through whatever training you have undergone, of what your body is doing on stage and what it is conveying, you need to develop a deep and intimate appreciation of the movement of your facial features. This awareness will allow you to connect the inner and the outer and will hugely enhance your performance **as long as it is prompted by truthful emotional engagement**.

Fully understanding this, and trusting that what you're feeling is available to an audience, is often particularly difficult for actors who have worked a lot in musicals where there is generally a more direct performer – audience relationship and greater projection. If you're accustomed to working with a 'two-finger smile' (one wide enough that you can get two fingers between your teeth) you may well need to go through a period of recalibrating the connection between your inner and outer.

TRY IT: Sit in front of a mirror and experiment with moving parts of your face consciously to see how the tiniest movements register to the observer. Learn how subtle your changes in expression can be. Complement this by working from the inside out: look away momentarily and find an internal emotional state, then look back to see how it manifests itself on your face. Change the emotion and observe how this change translates itself.

Film yourself in close-up while imagining various situations that generate a variety of emotions in you. Perhaps relive some emotional moments from your past while ignoring the camera. Do this entirely internally with no attempt to express them on your face. In playback you will see how these emotions reveal themselves in your expression, nonetheless. Remember the camera comes so close you don't need to push or signal anything. Or, for that matter, suppress anything. But you need to learn as much as you can about the relationship between what you *feel* and what happens on your face.

16
PLAYING THE CAMERA

> The area immediately around the lens is the most powerful place to look because the audience can see into your soul. Moving your eyes is a natural response to what happens in the inner or outer world. When this happens within the area around the camera (the doughnut) the audience can fully empathize with what you are feeling.

The doughnut

This is probably the single most important chapter in this book. It's also quite technical. Even if it's a struggle, stick with it: you need to know and understand this stuff.

For all the reasons I laid out in the previous chapter, when we look at people, we look at their eyes. As soon as babies can focus, they look at people's eyes. Even dogs and cats, it's said even rats, look at people's eyes to read their intentions.

So as soon as you appear on screen, this is where the audience will be looking. Making your performance available to the audience means making sure they have access to your eyes. And this means keeping your gaze primarily in the area around the camera.

However, you are probably also aware that you should never look straight **at** the camera unless explicitly told to by the director. The reason for this is simple: it breaks the fourth wall. One of the illusions of the screen is that we, the audience, can watch a character from very close up *without them knowing we're there*. As soon as the character looks down the lens, it feels as though they are looking directly at us and therefore the illusion is shattered.

So this gives us a ring-shaped area around the camera that respects the taboo of not looking directly at the audience but in which the eyes – the windows to the soul – remain accessible. I call this area *'the doughnut'* and working within it is the key to powerful screen acting (Figure 31).

Within the doughnut – windows to the soul open

Looking down the lens – breaking the fourth wall

Outside the doughnut – windows to the soul closed

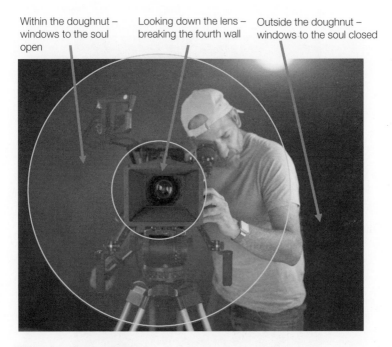

Figure 31 *'the doughnut'*.

Figures 32–34 show how looking in each of the three areas appears to the audience.

Figure 32 Looking down the lens – breaking the fourth wall.

Figure 33 Within the doughnut – windows to the soul open.

Figure 34 Outside the doughnut – windows to the soul closed.

During much of your time on screen you probably won't need to give any thought as to where you direct your eyes because your – the character's – attention is on some external stimulus, for example, another character, a sunset, a car that's backfired, someone in the distance, etc. Off-screen characters will be positioned by the director or camera operator so your eyes can be seen, and with things that are not actually physically there, you'll probably be told where to look. (If not, *ask*.)

But there will also be moments when your attention is on internal stimuli – you're just thinking. Most commonly, this will be when you're in a dialogue with another character and you break eye contact to consider what's just been said or think how to respond (remember, working on camera is about *re*acting as much as acting). Unless you, or the director, choose that the audience should not have access to your inner world (and this is a perfectly legitimate artistic choice), you should be looking roughly between the inner and outer circles of the doughnut because outside this area, it does not matter how profound or intense your emotion, the audience has no access to it and they are simply witnessing somebody having an experience they cannot share.

For a wonderful example of this look at the scene towards the end of episode 4 of *Breaking Bad* series 2 in which Skylar confronts Walt about his lying to her. It's a pivotal moment in their relationship and in Walt's descent into his moral quagmire. Both actors play the scene superbly, but Bryan Cranston makes the whole of his experience available to the camera by playing within the doughnut, whereas Anna Gunn drops out at times and becomes temporarily inaccessible to us. The difference is subtle but significant.

It's impossible to be precise about how large the doughnut is. It will depend on the lighting, the depth of your eye sockets, the prominence of your brow and several other factors that you cannot control. It's also not a straightforward question of being in or out. Rather, as you look further away from the camera, your eyes become less accessible until, eventually, we cannot see anything meaningful of them.

(Even if it were possible to be precise about where boundaries are for an individual actor, I would still want to discourage you from thinking too precisely about positioning because your inner monologue would then be the actor's, rather than the character's.)

Rather than working within the doughnut as a purely mechanical technique, the best way to think about it is to couple it with the desire to share your experience with the audience and look *in the vicinity of* the camera.

And, by the way, *'the doughnut'* is not a term that's in standard use within the industry. So don't expect someone else to understand what you mean by it unless they've been a student of mine or have read this book.

TRY IT: What follows is the first of a number of exercises to explore how to use eye movement on camera. Film yourself doing each one and play it back. If you don't have access to something that will record, you can do the exercises anyway – designate a real object as an imaginary camera and try to notice what happens to your eyes, although this is not as useful because your attention will inevitably be split as you do the exercise.

Think of something about which you feel strongly and improvise a bit of a rant about it. If you have a friend who's willing to be on the receiving end, then great. But if you don't, then tell an imaginary person. You'll very likely find that you break eye contact at times as you think of what to say next or pause for breath.

Try it again, but see if you can keep your eyes within the doughnut. In playback you'll see how much more accessible your inner world is.

Eye movement

I've already argued that the movement of our eyes reflects our inner thoughts and emotions and I want to return to the observation that, in life, our attention is either *out there* – seeking information – or *in here* – processing and reflecting. Specifically the *in here* bit is often accompanied by our gazing into the middle distance. These are the moments when, sitting on a train, we find ourselves staring into the lap of the person opposite us. We are not really looking at them. Mentally we're miles away.

Sometimes, as we're doing this, our eyes move involuntarily. It seems this helps us reflect. For example, if you watch somebody who is thinking through possible courses of action, you will often see their eyes flit from side to side.

If you've come across neurolinguistic programming (NLP), you will be familiar with the idea that our eyes move in different directions according to what we're doing. While I'm happy to believe that there is some truth in this – try it yourself – I don't think it's particularly helpful for an actor to treat NLP as anything more than an interesting observation about the link between the inner and outer. Certainly an actor who starts making deliberate choices about which way to look to reflect his character's thinking has stepped firmly into the territory of indicating.

I hope it's clear that what I'm suggesting is something entirely different: *'sharing'* instead of *'showing'*. If your inner monologue is a calculation of where to look, then that is what the audience will see. Whereas, if your inner monologue is the character's, relating to his hopes and aspirations, your eyes will automatically move appropriately. So let your inner impulses, derived from living truthfully in the imaginary circumstances, dictate your eye movements. All you need to do is to make sure that these naturally occurring eye movements remain within the doughnut.

TRY IT: Film yourself going through each of the following scenarios in your mind. Place the camera slightly to one side so you're not looking down the lens. Start by looking ahead and commit yourself to imagining the situation as fully as possible, letting your gaze go where it wants to.

After you've done them in order, watch it back and observe what your eyes do. You might also want to go back and try each one with your eyes deliberately looking to the side and/or up or down and see whether certain movements make things easier or harder.

1   Imagine yourself taking a euphoric curtain call at a theatre where you'd love to work, having played your dream part. Visualize a standing ovation sweeping through the auditorium.

2   Imagine being interviewed by an attractive and admiring journalist about the same performance and why you love the play.

3   Remember the last production you actually performed in. Picture the stage and the set.

4   Remember an embarrassing moment from your childhood. Identify where you were, what happened and how it made you feel.

5   Imagine someone you really fancy making an advance towards you. Imagine what they might do and how you might respond?

6   Recall an occasion when you felt angry either with a person or about an issue. If it's with a person, try to picture him and what he said or did that angered you. If it's about an issue, where were you when you felt the anger? What could you see and hear?

7   Recall the voice of your mother or someone significant from your childhood. Try to hear the tones of the voice.

8   Imagine your phone rings and you hear your favourite movie star introducing himself and asking you to come and meet him for a part in his next film, which he's producing.

You will probably find that your eyes naturally move as you imagine or remember. And you may see that depending on where your gaze goes, your inner world becomes more or less visible.

Do the exercise again and explore different eye movements. If some of them lead your eyes to travel downwards or away from the camera, try simultaneously allowing your eyes to move naturally, but within the range of the doughnut.

Knowing and not-knowing

Our lives are filled with moments when we learn things we did not previously know and go from a state of *not-knowing* to *knowing*. Most of these moments are banal. You tell me something fairly inconsequential, perhaps that you've bought a new phone cover. I now know that you have a new phone cover whereas, a moment ago, I didn't. Hardly earth shattering.

But drama, by definition, focuses on the dramatic and the revelations characters meet are frequently more significant. The enormously successful Hollywood screenwriter, William Goldman, writes in his wonderful book *Adventures in the Screen Trade* that most scenes start halfway through and end three-quarters of the way through. By this he means that in almost every scene something changes for the main character of the scene. Most scenes start just before this moment and end just after it.

In this moment – if you're lucky enough to be the main character in a scene – you hear something that changes your world and moves you closer to, or further away from, your goal. And if you are not the main character, the scene will probably still contain a number of moments when you go from *not-knowing* to *knowing*. Even if another character says something unsurprising, you go from a state of not-knowing to knowing. When this knowledge has consequences for you, it will frequently cause your eyes to move. These eye movements are very telling on camera and need to be contained within the doughnut so the audience can access your inner world.

Looking down

Let's look at how playing the doughnut works for a specific, and very common example of eye movement: looking down.

When we hear news – something that privately upsets or pleases or concerns us – we will frequently glance downwards with our eyes as we consider the consequences and ask ourselves questions like: *'How will it affect me?'* and *'How should I respond?'*

Playing the doughnut in these moments means glancing downwards with just your eyes, so that your gaze rests somewhere around the throat of the other character, instead of tilting your head and looking down towards the ground. Emotionally this feels pretty much the same as looking down, as long as it's prompted by the same impulse and the timing is dictated by your emotional reaction. But the audience's experience is totally different. Instead of you effectively disappearing behind your eyelids, they can still see you. Instead of witnessing, from outside, somebody having a response they can only really guess at, they can fully empathize with your experience.

Figures 35–40 show what it looks like when an actor looks down by different degrees, in relation to the camera lens.

Figure 35 POV of actress, camera and tripod.

Figure 36 Eye contact with actress: Hearing news.

Figure 37 Digesting news – eyes to A – internal reaction fully visible.

Figure 38 Digesting news – eyes to B – internal reaction less visible.

Figure 39 Digesting news – eyes to C – internal reaction hard to see.

Figure 40 Digesting news – eyes to D – internal reaction no longer visible.

As you can see, the further down the actor looks, the less we can see of her eyes. (I should add that this holds true for any news that creates an internal reaction, not only bad news.)

Let's be clear about this, simply looking down, with no emotional engagement, is not likely to fool anyone. Unlike on stage, where a truthfully conceived and skilfully executed physical movement can convincingly convey what the character is feeling, even if the actor is not directly experiencing it, for example, gasping in shock or turning away when rejected.

Because the camera comes so close, and because we can all thin-slice when reading faces, what's happening behind your eyes has to be real. The point of keeping your eyes within the doughnut is that it allows us to *see*. So you must commit yourself to the scene, fully engage with what's happening externally and internally and allow it to affect you, but couple your truthful responses with the desire to share your experience with the camera. If you can do this, then playing the doughnut will come naturally and your eye movements will be spontaneous and revealing.

TRY IT: Imagine someone telling you about the death of someone you care about. Then imagine someone telling you you've got a fantastic part in a film in both cases focus on your internal reaction – how you *feel* – rather than creating a visible reaction and *doing* something for the benefit of your imaginary partner (or the camera).

See where your eyes naturally go. Then do it again deliberately letting your eyes drop a little but staying within the doughnut.

Lateral eye movement

Another very characteristic response to the move from *not-knowing* to *knowing* is a brief sideways movement of the eyes. Examining this carries further risk of seeming to offer a technical gimmick to help you fake your way through a screen performance, though I'm sure it's clear by now that's not what I'm suggesting.

When faced with new information, we frequently break eye contact with the speaker, look slightly to one side for a beat, then look back to hear more. In essence, it's the journey from *out there* to *in here* – as we consider what we've just heard and what it means for us – then back *out there* again to seek further information.

Containing this within the doughnut often involves choosing to look closer to the camera (Figures 41–43) – or even across to the other side

Figure 41 Looking at partner.

Figure 42 Breaking eye contact and gazing into the distance *within the doughnut*.

Figure 43 Looking back at partner.

of the camera – rather than looking away from the camera where it's not visible (Figures 44–46).

Figure 44 Looking at partner.

Figure 45 Breaking eye contact and gazing into the distance *outside the doughnut*.

Figure 46 Looking back at partner.

You may intuitively recognize this – after all you've been doing it unconsciously all your life. And laid out like this it sounds very clinical and, followed slavishly, it will probably read on camera as contrived and anything but truthful. But in the cutting room, these small facial movements, especially of the eyes, are what directors use to reveal the characters to the audience. Learning to contain your eye movements within the doughnut, and therefore allowing the audience access to your inner world, is a very important part of making the transition from the stage to the screen.

For a masterclass in eye movement by two giants of screen acting, check out the famous coffee shop scene in *Heat*, with Al Pacino's cop going head to head with Robert de Niro's bank robber.

TRY IT: Imagine there is someone in front of you who tells you something unexpected. Make it somebody specific, revealing something specific. Nothing earth-shattering but something that nevertheless has consequences for you – perhaps your agent tells you he's quitting. Immediately after you imagine he's said it, try looking to the side for a moment – using just your eyes – as you consider what this means for you, and then look back, wanting to know more: Is it definite? When will it happen? What will happen next? Experiment with looking slightly to the side of your imaginary person (inside the doughnut) and then looking way over to the side (outside the doughnut).

Now try it again and try breaking eye contact *across* the camera to the other side from your imaginary partner. This is incredibly effective on camera.

Repeated eye movements

These eye moments don't only happen in response to what others say and do. You might be doing the talking and momentarily break eye contact as you go *in here* to think or to search for the right words for what you want to say. We rarely look at other people for prolonged periods of time even if we like them and the exchange is going well. Rather, we tend to look at people, then look away and look back, look away and look back, continually throughout most interactions. Each time he looks away, the screen actor needs to keep his eyes largely within the doughnut so the audience can share in his internal world.

Something really significant happening internally might give rise to protracted lateral eye movement, for example, when we realize something or wrestle with internal conflict.

A great example (spoiler alert!) occurs in *The Godfather* part I, as Michael Corleone (Al Pacino again) sits in a restaurant with two Mafiosi, trying to muster the courage to shoot them with the gun he has under the table. It's arguably the single most significant moment of the entire trilogy as Michael moves from law-abiding citizen, who has previously rejected the family business, to murderous crime boss.

As he grapples with doubt and contemplates the consequences of what he's about to do, Michael withdraws completely from the external world – he's entirely *in here*. The camera pushes in on his face, the voices of the Mafiosi fade out and the sound ramps up the screeches of trains entering a nearby station. Pacino's eyes dart frantically to and fro as he struggles with his decision. He then re-enters the *out there* in spectacular fashion as he pulls the trigger.

Most of our engagement with the world, and with other people, is a more dynamic mixture of *out there* and *in here* as our attention flits between the two landscapes. We go backwards and forwards, continually seeking information, repeatedly going from *not-knowing* to *knowing*, and considering how this knowledge affects us,

The significance of the timing of eye movement can't be overstated. In the same way that we can tell whether someone is truly listening to us merely from the timing of when they say *'yes'*, the timing of when people move their eyes and where they look reveals their thoughts.

TRY IT: Imagine you discover that the partner of your best friend is having an affair and you must decide whether or not to tell him. Make up whatever circumstances you need to make the decision as difficult as possible. Then film yourself wrestling with the decision, moving your eyes as you think through the arguments and possible consequences.

The full subtlety and complexity of working the doughnut is almost impossible to describe using words alone, so I have recorded a demonstration of a small part of it on my website billbritten.co.uk/stagetoscreen

17
LOVING THE CAMERA

> Many professional actors are frightened of the camera but you must
> learn to love it if it is to love you. Practise this.

Loving the camera

Lots of professional actors are, in their hearts, frightened of the camera.
It sits there on its tripod, dominating the proceedings, fussed over and
fetishized by a group of (usually) burly men and judging the poor actor's
performance. Worse, it is all seeing. It scrutinizes everything you do,
peering into your core and exposing any lapse in concentration or hint
of untruthfulness.

If this is how you feel, I sympathize. For stage actors particularly,
accustomed to being the centre of attention and able to sense their
audience's response in a collaborative communion, the camera's coldness
and detachment can be forbidding and intimidating. But you must learn
to get over it. The camera **is** your audience. And you know how a theatre
audience feels about an actor who either despises or fears it.

An actor who is intimidated by the camera will always carry an edge
of tension that will undermine the best performance. By comparison, if
you carefully watch the great screen actors, you will see that they love
the camera. Helen Mirren, for example, patently adores it. Not in an
egotistical, show-off way. Rather, she really wants the camera – and
through it, the audience – to share in what she is experiencing.

One of the most telling indications of whether an actor loves the camera, or is intimidated by it, is whether they break eye contact towards or away from the camera. An actor who is frightened by the camera will unconsciously choose to look away from it, in the same way that we avoid looking at someone in the room who scares us. Whereas an actor who loves the camera will frequently break eye contact towards and sometimes even across it, keeping their gaze within the doughnut and their inner world open to the audience.

> **Anthony Hopkins:** *'You have to have a respect for the camera, a real respect, and a real love for it.'*

The suggestion that you could look across the camera, might even fill you with a slight sense of panic. Many actors fear they will accidentally look down the lens and if this is the case for you, I would not recommend experimenting with it on a paying job. Don't try to run before you can walk.

The technical facility to play within the doughnut is built on an internal wish to share your inner world with the audience. In an earlier chapter I used the analogy of convex and concave. The idea behind the notion of a concave performance is that it invites the audience into the character's inner world. Underpinning this, I believe, is a generosity of spirit: love.

I'm well aware that it's easier to say *'love the camera'* than to do it and I wish there were some miraculous way to make this happen. But it is something you must patiently work on by practising on your own in a no-risk environment. The worst place to do this is on the job, watched by the director and surrounded by the crew and your fellow actors.

I've already suggested you get yourself a camcorder. If you need to work on loving the camera, then get one that looks like a camera rather than a phone because the point is to have something that represents *'camera'*, the repository of your fears and anxieties, rather than simply a recording device. Ideally get a simple tripod too – again they are dirt cheap. If you really cannot afford a camera, use your phone. Film yourself acting, over and over again, and watch the results on the biggest monitor you have access to (the director will be watching your performance on a large, super sharp monitor. And if you're cast in a film, the audience may be watching you on a screen 20 metres across).

What you should work towards is the idea of sharing. You – as your character – are having an experience during a scene. Share it. Let the audience in. Make it available to them. And, without doing anything as active as *'sending'*, open yourself emotionally to the camera.

TRY IT: Ideally set up a camera on a tripod in front of you and slightly off to one side. If you don't have one, then identify any object that you can think of as the *camera*. Now look straight ahead at a different object directly in front of you. Try to block out the camera from your thoughts and focus solely on the object. Noticing all the detail in it may help you with this.

Now, without removing your gaze from this object, allow the camera into your consciousness, but with warmth. Imagine it's someone you love and who loves you and always sees the good in you – your mother perhaps, or a lover or close friend. Imagine this person smiling encouragingly. Now imagine a golden light emanating from the camera, bathing you in its glow, making you feel special. Try to feel the space around the camera as warm and light and inviting.

Now, still looking at the object in front of you, put your attention on the space to the other side, away from the camera. Imagine that space as cold and dark and uncomfortable.

All the time looking at the object in front of you, move your attention backwards and forwards between the space around the camera and the space to the other side of the object. See if you can reinforce in yourself that sense of warmth and light versus cold and dark.

If you've read through the last few paragraphs, understanding them intellectually but not actually doing the exercise, then go back and read it again but stopping after each paragraph and doing what it describes.

Do this every day for a month and see what changes take place for you. If you were to film yourself in the same scene at the beginning and the end of the month, I suspect you'd see a considerable difference in the tonal quality of your relationship with the camera.

Another way of looking at this is to imagine it's one of those days when it's warm in the sunshine but quite cold in the shade. You will find yourself naturally turning your face to the sun in preference to turning away from the sun. If you were to compare the same conversation with the same person in the sun or in the shade (let's just assume everything else – mood, context, timing etc. – is the same) nothing would change other than your orientating yourself slightly differently in relation to the sun. This is very different to having the same conversation with a third person observing, where what you do and say – your *intention* – would be affected.

Or perhaps, the camera could represent someone you trust rather than the sun? I once directed a lovely older actress who asked me one day why I did not call 'action'. The answer was that early in my career, I worked with a particularly difficult 1st AD who insisted he should be the one to call 'action'. At the time it did not seem a battle worth fighting (there were others) so I got into the habit of leaving it to the 1st, while I would call 'cut'. *'Does it matter?'* I asked the actress and she replied that it mattered a lot. For many years she had been frightened of the camera. Giving the director her performance through the camera was her technique for overcoming this fear. When the 1st called 'action' it simply meant *'everything is ready. Start now.'* But when I called 'action' it meant *'I'm here for you and ready to receive your performance'*.

Loving the camera is primarily about an attitude rather than an external, physical orientation. There are occasional moments when turning your head or even your body towards, rather than away from, the camera can help the audience share your experience. But, more often, allowing your eyes to play in the doughnut derives from your emotional engagement with the camera.

SECTION THREE

DOING IT

18
GETTING THE JOB

The director is looking to cast someone who is the character rather than someone who can act the character. To maximize your chances of getting the job, prepare thoroughly, turn up on time and be friendly. The casting director may read badly so decide how to play the scene beforehand. Some of the decision-makers will only see the recorded footage so hold up the script and play the doughnut.

Castings

Just as in the theatre, getting a job is an art in itself. And it's only loosely related to your ability to do the job once you've got it.

There are two main things to understand when it comes to castings for screen work, both very different to theatre auditions.

The first is that directors are looking for verisimilitude. That is, they are looking for the real thing rather than someone who can *act* the thing.

The basic question a theatre director is trying to answer in an audition is: *'How good an actor is he?'* Can this person in front of me, over the course of several weeks' rehearsal, use imagination, insight and stage technique to create and perform a character that is original and compelling? And in part you, the actor, are trying to convince the director of your acting – your transformational – ability.

The screen director simply doesn't have time on set for any of this. He assumes that if you've been put in front of him by a casting director then you have a basic ability to speak lines as though you've just thought of them, rather than sounding like a script. But he doesn't want potential, he wants to see what he will get if he hires you.

He will be seeing a stream of people for the role and his perfect actor is probably one he doesn't have to direct at all, someone who'll just deliver with a minimum of fuss. You're a commodity and until you are well enough known that he can make a judgement on your transformational ability from your previous work (and by this I mean stuff he's seen just because he's seen it, rather than having to make a special effort to seek it out – he doesn't have time), you need to offer something that doesn't involve a leap of faith.

Now you can carp all you like about lack of imagination, but the director will be under intense pressure to meet the schedule so why would he take the risk of backing a promise if he has the option of casting someone who actually *is* (or appears to be) the character? This does not mean you should go hell for leather to impersonate the character from the moment you walk through the door – that way you will diminish the likelihood of his considering you for anything else – but I would suggest you tilt your self-presentation towards the character.

The second big difference is that most of the people involved in the casting decision, certainly in television, will not be in the room. Unless you are dealing with a star director who has temporarily stepped down from a successful movie career to direct an authored piece, there will be several producers, executive producers, commissioning editors and channel controllers participating in any casting decision and the final say will usually belong to an executive, not the director. First, the project will only get green-lit if there are name actors attached (or, very occasionally a name writer or director) because this is what will determine whether it gets an initial audience. But sadly, this increasingly means the casting of the smaller parts also rests with the most senior executive. And in a movie, there will also be numerous producers and executive producers who are at least consulted. These people are too busy to meet you and anyway they're not concerned with how the performance will happen – that's the director's job. But they will view the footage because they are interested in what you will deliver. And unfortunately, the process of recording your reading is not reliably helpful to your chances.

The casting will usually take place as follows: you're asked, often at less than a day's notice, to attend at a given time and place. You may have your availability checked some days or weeks before this. Being asked whether you are available does **not** mean you will necessarily be interviewed. It's part of the process by which casting directors draw up a shortlist of people for the director to see.

If you are called in to meet the director, you will usually be sent the script beforehand, although sometimes you will only get to see it when you arrive for your appointment.

You meet the director and the casting director who spend a few minutes chatting with you. They will ask you if you would mind reading, to which your answer will be an enthusiastic *'I'd love to'*. You'll read the part, with the other parts read by the casting director. The director might then ask you to read it again, with a little bit of direction, or he will have seen enough, in which case he'll thank you and say his goodbyes. This will typically take 10 minutes or less because all they really want is to get a sense of you as a person and get a reading down on camera to show the executives.

Improving the odds

First things first: be prepared. This is your opportunity to get work, so give yourself the best chance. This means doing your homework. If you have been sent the whole script, read it. Understand the whole piece, its style and genre, and how your character fits into it. Read it again.

Learn the lines for any scenes you've been asked to prepare. Thoroughly. Knowing your lines does not make you desperate (we all know how unattractive desperation is in an actor), it makes you professional. No director ever decided not to give an actor a job because he had learnt the lines.

Prepare the character thoroughly – I address how to do this in the chapters on preparation. You should do the work but hold it very lightly because if the director wants you to do something different when you read, you need to be able to adapt readily. However, in the first instance you are trying to offer something vivid and rich and thorough and character preparation will help you do this.

Unlike the preparation for the shoot itself, I suggest you do explore specific interpretations of lines and perhaps even decide how to play things. I'll come to this shortly.

Being prepared also means being on time and in the right emotional space. The casting is the most important thing you will do that day and being late or running errands on the way there or making that difficult phone call just before you go in will not help you get the job.

If you have not been sent the script in advance, get there early. By which I mean at least an hour. I now recognize that I lost myself numerous acting jobs by arriving just a few minutes before my appointment, speed-reading the script a couple of times and then proceeding to do a terrible casting, not only deterring the director from hiring me, but also convincing the casting director not to waste any more directors' time by bringing me in again.

Contrast this with an experience I had as a director. When casting the guest lead part of a 15-year-old boy, in an episode of a long-running series, there was only a small pool of possibilities in terms of appropriate age range, qualities and experience. One young-looking, recent drama school graduate stood out head and shoulders above the others but had no screen experience. However, he did a fantastic reading, totally off-book despite not having had had the script sent to him beforehand. When I asked the casting director's assistant about him, she told me he'd arrived an hour and a half early, taken the script away (during which time he'd evidently learnt it) and returned 15 minutes before his appointed time. This professionalism completely neutralized any concerns about his lack of screen experience. He got the job (the execs approved) and gave a great performance.

The point is not just that he was manifestly professional; his reading was so much better than the others because of how prepared he was.

Having got there early, be personable. Be pleasant to any receptionists or assistants. Not only does this make the world a nicer place for everybody to live in, but they may be asked their opinion about you. And it's possible that, in years to come, they might become influential casting directors themselves.

Be prepared for the fact that you will probably walk into a waiting room full of people exactly like you, but slightly better-looking and more charismatic. Remember they would not have brought you in if they did not think you were a possibility. I'm bald and I had to get used to walking into a room full of bald men because the less imaginative casting directors will latch onto any physical description and bring in a clutch of actors who match it. Equally, if you walk into a room full of actors who are identical and totally different to you, that's fine too: you are the wild card. Dustin Hoffman's breakthrough part in *The Graduate* was famously written for a standard romantic lead which, in 1967, meant a tall, square-jawed WASP, not a short, neurotic Jew with a big nose. Hoffman nonetheless got seen and got the part. (And, it's worth noting that after this imaginative piece of casting, he didn't try to emulate the character described in the script. Instead he made the part very much his own, while still playing out the story.)

You should also be prepared for the fact that you will probably be kept waiting. Despite my stressing the importance of your being punctual, this will not always be reciprocated. Casting directors allow only a very short amount of time for each actor and many directors feel, as I used to, that (a) it's rude to rush people through and (b) they need slightly longer to explore what an actor can bring. Therefore they run late.

The good news is that people will usually be polite to you, in complete contrast to the casual disrespect with which you are treated more generally, for example, being expected to be available at very short notice and then kept waiting. Despite how it may feel, this disrespect is not actually deliberate. Most of those who work in the industry are, in my experience, decent people who want to behave well, but they are wrestling with fantastically short deadlines and tight budgets. The fact is you *can* put out a casting call at 5.00 one evening to see actors at 9.00 the following morning and have a string of skilled, willing professionals turn up, eager to get the job.

While you wait to be seen, everything I've said elsewhere about getting yourself into the right frame of mind, and keeping yourself there, applies. Chat to the other actors if it will help you prepare. Don't, if it doesn't. If you see another actor you know, the same applies. If he wants to chat, and you don't, explain that you need to concentrate on the script, and arrange to meet him afterwards. Turn your phone off. Do not check your emails. You are there to get work and the administration of your life can wait.

In the room

Once you get in the room, there is an etiquette to be followed which usually begins with a few minutes of chat – *'how did you get here?'*

'where do you live?' 'what have you been doing recently?'. Its purpose is not actually to satisfy a curiosity about your travel arrangements or your part-time bar job any more than *'how are you?'* is an enquiry about your health. They just want to hear you talk and get a sense of you as a person. The director also wants to form some sense of whether you are likely to be 'difficult' should you get the job. So play your part and chat amiably, even if it feels inane. One of my biggest mistakes as a young actor was to revert to the state of a truculent and monosyllabic 14-year-old when faced with these questions. This did not help me get work. Normal conversational etiquette applies, so do NOT respond to *'how are you?'* with a discourse on your current ailments. Making a fleeting reference to the head cold that has now more or less cleared up is as far as you should go and a safer option is *'fine, thanks'*. And this etiquette is, of course, one way, so don't enquire about their health or how the meetings with other actors have been going. Let them ask the questions.

One of the most difficult aspects of these pleasantries is if they fly in the face of what the role requires you to do. If you have spent the previous hour working yourself up into a state of rage in order to play an angry character or reliving some personal trauma for the part of someone troubled, it can be very difficult to turn this off and then on again. I wish there were some easy answer to this conundrum but there isn't. More sensitive directors will recognize that you're braced to read and help you with this. Less sensitive ones – and there are many – don't and won't.

When it comes to the reading, be prepared for the fact that the casting director will probably appear to have been on a special training course at which he learnt how to read badly. When auditioning actors, it never ceased to amaze me the incompetence with which many casting directors would mumble, stumble, hesitate and read with no feeling whatsoever. The only meaningful explanation I can offer for this, and for any insensitivity on the part of the director, either in the casting or on set, is that they don't really understand what actors do. They recognize brilliance when they see it and they know there are certain things that will inhibit an actor's performance, but the rest is a bit of a mystery.

This is why I suggested earlier that you make some decisions in advance about how to play the scene. The executives watching the footage will not make any allowances for poor reading by someone off-camera and they all want to see something strongly imagined and vivid. So reacting to how you *imagine* the other character might have spoken the lines is the best way to go if you're not getting much from whoever is reading, because your aim is to get the job, not to create great art for posterity. And doing this is easier if you have done so as part of your preparation. At the very least you need to imagine that the off-screen character has engaged with you.

Remember as you are reading that most of the people involved in the decision will only see you on the recording. Play the doughnut. This can be the hardest thing to do because you're so focused on impressing the people in the room with you. But everything I've written about playing the camera is incredibly important. If you are *reading* (Figure 47), then you must hold the piece of paper up so your eyes can be seen on camera (Figure 48). Ideally, look at the person you're reading opposite and glance down at the paper when you need to, rather than having your eyes glued to the paper throughout (Figure 49). This really will make a huge difference. Record yourself reading – and I mean *literally* reading – and see for yourself in the playback. It's completely uninteresting because your eyes are not visible. Then record yourself reading but looking at your partner for most of it and glancing down occasionally and you'll see what a huge difference it makes.

Oddly, the camera sometimes gets placed way off to the side to give a really poor angle on you. I even once failed to get the actor I wanted cast because his reading had been done at a different time to the other contenders and the camera had been placed off to the side so nothing much registered on the recording. The execs refused to accept my assurance that my chosen actor had given the best reading and they went with someone from the first casting session instead, simply because they could see his eyes.

Asking for the camera to be moved is tricky without looking like a wise-guy and alienating the casting director. But you might be able to do so – *'I'd like to be able to include the camera'* – with enough charm to get away with it. If not, then try to orientate yourself a little towards it. Literally turn your body so you're angled towards it, as if it were a theatre audience. This means that when you break eye contact with the person reading, your eyes will naturally move in the right direction – towards camera.

Figure 47 Reading, holding the paper down.

Figure 48 Reading, holding the paper up.

Figure 49 Look at the casting director and glance down occasionally.

Regardless of the camera's positioning, find moments to break eye contact when your character might be thinking about what he has just heard and PLAY THE DOUGHNUT.

Take your leave graciously when it's indicated that the meeting is over. Don't interpret too much from whether or not the director asks you to read again. Being asked means he hasn't decided *against* casting you but sometimes, as director, you know the person is right and there's no point in prolonging the meeting, especially when you're half an hour behind and have others waiting to be seen.

If you feel your reading was really poor and you know you can do better, there's no harm in asking to read again even if you're not invited to. Personally, my inclination was always to let an actor do so if he wanted to, although casting directors occasionally tried to prevent this as they tried to keep me on track timewise. But if you do this, make sure your second reading is substantially better or at least different. You could even lose yourself a job you might otherwise have got by merely repeating your first attempt, because it demonstrates that you have no real control over what you're doing. What it suggests is that you might be one of those actors who wastes everyone's time on set by always wanting to do another take but without actually doing it better when allowed to.

Before you go, make sure you look the director and the casting director in the eye, shake their hands and thank them for seeing you. I don't mean make a song and dance of this. Do it lightly, but do it nonetheless. Confident but gracious is what you're aiming for. This is the impression of yourself that you'll leave behind and no one ever objects to someone who's courteous and appreciative.

Once you've left the room, let it go: assume you haven't got the job and get on with your life. I know this is hard to do but most of the time you won't hear anything back at all and constantly wondering whether you got jobs will drive you insane. Sometimes it can take ages for a decision to be made because of all the people who have to be consulted. Sometimes it's later the same day. Sometimes it's offered to someone else who declines or pulls out later and they come to you weeks later. It's all chaotic and unpredictable and unfathomable, so you have to learn some sort of inner calm about the absurdity of the business. The bottom line is that if you're an actor looking to work for others, you are absolutely at their mercy, along with the thousands of other hopefuls. So you will be blown about like a dandelion seed.

Having let go of whether or not you got the job it is, however, worth spending a little time reflecting on how you handled the meeting and if there's anything to learn from it. I'm a great believer in this kind of reflection. There's no doubt there are some actors who are very good indeed at the process of getting work and they're not always the ones who deliver the best performances on set.

While there are no simple solutions, as I mentioned earlier, the one thing that is guaranteed not to get you the job is desperation. In this respect it's a bit like dating. And of course desperation is very hard to hide. Avoiding it is another book entirely. To desperation I'd add anger and rudeness as casting-wrecking qualities though, oddly, arrogance can be a plus for some roles.

Filming yourself for castings

The initial stages of casting are increasingly being done by asking selected actors to film themselves reading scenes and send the footage to the casting director. When you consider that the director is only really interested initially in seeing an actor read, this makes sense, sparing him the time and energy required to meet lots of actors, most of whom simply won't be right for the role. He can then meet a more targeted selection of actors face to face.

As the technology gets ever better this will become more and more attractive so you will need to master some of the basics of filming. Fundamentally, what they are interested in is your performance, not wonderful production values, but there's a certain minimum standard you need to achieve in order to let them see what you're offering.

First, learn the lines. Why deliver a reading when you have the opportunity to deliver a performance that is much more likely to get you through to the next round of casting?

Second, make sure the shot is close enough. A distant shot that shows your entire body as well as much of the room you're in, is just making it harder for anyone watching it to see what they really want, which is your face. So go for a loose medium close-up (MCU) (Figure 5).

Third, place the camera on a flat surface. Ideally use a tripod, but if you don't have one, or you're using a mobile phone, you don't want your footage recorded at an angle. Best is to place it slightly below your own eyes, about level with, say, your mouth because it elevates your stature. This is the default positioning of the camera in movies and explains why even famously short actors seem taller on screen than in real life: the audience is literally looking up at the hero.

Fourth, make sure you are easily audible. Most camcorders have decent enough sound if you film yourself in a quiet room. But ambient sound often registers far louder on a recording than you hear it at the time. So before you put your all into your performance, do a test recording. It's very frustrating to do 25 takes, until you're finally happy with your performance, only to discover that the sound quality isn't good enough.

Fifth, consider the background of your shot. It's only really important in terms of there being nothing distracting in it: no other people, nothing moving about, no potted plant appearing to grow out of the side of your head, etc.

Sixth, get someone off-camera to read the other character's lines and place this person close to the camera to bring your eyeline round.

Seventh, take the time and trouble to commit yourself emotionally to the scene so that your performance is as good as it can possibly be, rather than allowing yourself to be distracted by the process of filming yourself. This is a job interview, so take it seriously.

And lastly, make sure you send your footage in a format that can be easily viewed. If necessary, ring the casting director's office (or ask your agent to do it) to find out exactly what format they'd like. If they can't easily open yours, they're not going to put themselves out trying to convert it. There are too many other actors to be seen.

There's no need to edit it, except to take out irrelevances at the start and end, for example, your friend telling you that the camera's recording or you heavy breathing to psych yourself up. There are many free-to-download programmes that will allow you to do this. Do NOT get clever by editing different takes together or, even worse, showing off your editing skills with dissolves, wipes or whatever trickery you have mastered. The director is not looking for an editor: he just wants to see you portray another human being.

I'd encourage you to see this as an opportunity, rather than something to resent. Apart from anything else, many others will send in something pretty poor. You would be amazed at how amateur many people's efforts are and it's not hard to stand out if you put a little effort into it.

19
PREPARATION

> You must do all the preparation work of a theatre rehearsal and more, by yourself, until you have a vivid, deeply imagined character.

Creating a character

So you've got the job, got the script and it's time to prepare. There are many similarities between the preparation required for the screen and what you would do in a theatre rehearsal period. But two things differ: first, because there's almost no rehearsal, the exploration, preparation and planning has to be done alone and secondly, you need to refrain from making decisions about how you'll play the scene.

First let's explore the question of character. Just consider yourself as life finds you right now. You know who you are. You could describe to me your childhood, where you grew up and the major events that have formed the person you are. You know whom you like and dislike, whom you admire and whom you despise, what your relationship is - or was like with your parents and other members of your family. You could tell me about the relationships that are important to you now, precisely, person by person. You know what you enjoy. You know whom you envy and what makes you jealous. You know what your ambitions are. You may be confident of achieving them or painfully aware of the gap between them and what you think will actually come to pass.

You are located somewhere in space and time. You could say where you are without raising your eyes from the page. You could say how you got there and how long you have been there. You could describe what has happened to you, or what you read, in the last 10 minutes. You could tell me where you were half an hour ago, what you did this morning and what you plan to do later today. You could say what troubles you and what you are looking forward to tomorrow, next week and next month.

All this and much, much more goes to make up the three-dimensional person that you are, with a vivid and richly contoured inner life, and you carry this everywhere with you. People who meet you will get a sense of some of these things in you. They won't perceive all of it, but some of it will be there implicitly, influencing how you speak and walk and behave and engage with other human beings.

This is what the audience needs to sense when you appear on screen: a fully realized person with hopes, dreams, fears, longings, concerns and so on.

If you're lucky, your character will have his own narrative arc with a dramatically interesting objective and actions you can play. But even if your role is relatively functional, every human being is the hero of his own life story, and we can instantly tell the difference between an actor going through the motions in order to service somebody else's storyline and a real person whose own journey through the world happens to collide with one of the characters in the story we are following.

Of course, all this applies in the theatre, and you may well take it for granted that this is part of the preparation you do for any role in any medium. But think for a moment about the intense scrutiny of the camera and your own ability to thin-slice. Have you ever found yourself talking to somebody and experienced a moment of real insight about what's going on for them? Perhaps a moment when somebody's eyes have misted over and you've realized that they are unexpectedly on the edge of tears? In this moment you caught a glimpse of what truly lies behind the mask, thanks to a combination of deep attention by you and unguarded vulnerability in them. I will guess that, if you have indeed experienced this, you were surely only a few feet from the person in question. It's not something that can be done at 20 paces.

This is the potential that the camera offers the actor. And even if your part does not appear to offer the opportunity to reveal your character in this way, you had better be ready for it nonetheless, because if your characterization is hollow, then that is what the audience will sense. It's also worth remembering that great actors can open up a whole hinterland of personal history and yearning with a single line or even a look. For a great example of this, watch the scene in the film *Michael Clayton* in which George Clooney's character listens to a hit-and-run driver justifying how he came to knock down a pedestrian. At a critical point in the driver's description, his wife, who is standing behind him, throws her whisky tumbler against the wall. In that moment the couple's entire marriage is laid bare. There's a terrific performance by Denis O'Hare as the driver but, without a single line of dialogue, Julie White also conveys a level of frustration and anger that tells you everything you need to know about their relationship.

As I discussed in the chapter on Listening, it's my belief that actors should not take prior decisions about what they will actually do during the scene. Prepare thoroughly, then throw it away and react to what happens in front of you.

If you decide in advance how you're going to play the scene, you are not seeking the connection with the other actors that makes a scene catch fire and you will struggle to respond truthfully. You also run the risk of being derailed if the director wants something else or the other actors do something unexpected, because your inner monologue will be focused on the gap between your plan and what is actually happening.

Doing your preparation entirely alone, before you show up on set, requires high levels of discipline and commitment. It's my observation that many young actors, even those who have been through an extensive drama school training, lack a methodology that enables them to do the depth of preparation that is needed for the screen, without the support structure of other actors and a rehearsal process.

So I will use the screenplay of the 1981 film *Body Heat* to explore some elements of preparation. I'm not offering a systematic approach. Actors vary hugely as to how they work and, in my opinion, there are no rights and wrongs. So I'd encourage you to start from your existing approach to preparation for a role in the theatre and incorporate ideas and techniques that seem useful.

I have chosen this film because (a) it's extremely well written and acted, (b) it's not so widely known that you are likely to have seen it and (c) although it was written in the 1980s, the dramatic scenario is not specific to the period. Be warned, however, that I will necessarily discuss the ending, and so spoil your enjoyment of a fine film. Nevertheless, I'd suggest you do not watch it before reading the following chapters. Once you've seen somebody else play a part on screen, it's very hard to rid your mind of his performance.

I'll start with the minor part of Teddy which, although he appears in only two scenes, was something of a breakthrough for the actor who played him. (I suggest you don't google it in case knowing who it was prejudices your ability to read the part fresh).

20
BODY HEAT – PLOT SYNOPSIS

First, let me give you a rough synopsis of the plot. Ned Racine is a lawyer in a mid-sized, middle-American town. He has dubious ethics, is a bit of a ladies' man and is bored. He meets and then pursues Matty, a devastatingly attractive, married woman with whom he starts an affair. She hates her wealthy husband, Edmund, and, before long, Racine suggests they kill him. Racine breaks into their house in the middle of the night, pretending to be a burglar, and, as they planned, kills Edmund when Matty sends him downstairs to investigate. Racine and Matty dump the body in a derelict property, The Breakers, that Edmund was buying with some shady business associates and start a fire, hoping the police will conclude that he was murdered by his partners and that the arson was an attempt to get rid of the evidence.

But when Edmund's will is read, Racine discovers that Matty changed it, shortly before they murdered him, to disinherit Edmund's sister, and forged Racine's signature as the witness. Racine slowly starts to suspect that Matty has planned the entire thing, including their initial 'chance' encounter, in order that Racine should kill Edmund and then take the blame, while she collects the entire inheritance.

At the denouement we discover that the imprisoned Racine is right. We never find out what truly happened but Racine's speculation is our best guess: Matty's real name was Mary Ann. She stole the identity of a school classmate, the real Matty, perhaps to distance herself from something terrible that she'd done. But the real Matty found out, possibly once 'Matty' was already married to Edmund, and was blackmailing her over it. 'Matty' had planned to kill both Racine and the real Matty (now calling herself 'Mary Ann') with a bomb in Edmund's boathouse. She knew that 'Mary Ann's' body would be identified, through dental records, as being Matty. So the police would conclude that a wealthy man had been killed by his wife and her lover – both of whom would then be dead – and close the case, leaving 'Matty' free to return to being Mary Ann or possibly, to adopt a new identity and enjoy her ill-gotten gains. (I know it's a little hard to follow, but that's the nature of film noir.)

And here are the two scenes in which Teddy appears.

INT. TEDDY LAURSEN'S WORKSHOP – NIGHT

TEDDY LAURSEN, rock'n roll arsonist, is keeping the beat and mouthing the words along with the Bruce Springsteen tape on his workbench. Teddy is in his mid-twenties, dressed in a black T-shirt and jeans. His arson workshop is located in the basement of an old building. All around him are the tools and supplies of his trade: wire, rope, cans, vises, alarm clocks, chemical containers, and a huge assortment of mechanical implements. He keeps all his small accessories in dozens of cigar boxes, unlabeled.

He knows where everything is. Teddy is watching Racine, who is kneeling on the floor before a compact incendiary device. Teddy winces at the way Racine clips two wires together. He reaches over to turn down the tape slightly, then squats down next to Racine to demonstrate the proper method.

                    TEDDY
          Whatsa matter, you can't think with
          a little music?
                    (demonstrating)
          Like this, I said.

Racine nods then duplicates the clipping. Teddy goes back to his stool, slapping the beat of the music on his thigh. Racine pulls out the alarm lever on the clock attached to the device and stands up. He throws a look to Teddy and Teddy nods that, yes, the device is now set.

                         RACINE
         That's it?

                          TEDDY
                   (nods to the music)
         It's fast. It's hot. It's simple.
         You can use the clock or rig it to
         something that moves. It starts
         big and it'll go with just the mag
         clips. If you want more, splash a
         little accelerator around.

                         RACINE
         Just regular gasoline?

                          TEDDY
         Regular, unleaded, supreme –
         whatever you like, counselor. I
         got to tell you, though, this mama
         has a big drawback.

                         RACINE
         What?

                          TEDDY
         It's easy to spot, even after the
         meltdown. They'll know it's arson.

                         RACINE
         I don't care about that.
                   (looks at Teddy)
         That's all there is to it?

Teddy is offended.

                          TEDDY
         No. No-no-no-no. That ain't all
         there is to it. You gotta get in,
         you gotta get out. You gotta pick
         the right spot and the right time.
         And you gotta try not to get famous
         while you're in the act.
                   (gestures at the
                        device)

If that was all there was to it,
any idiot could do it.

                    RACINE
Sorry.

                    TEDDY
Hey, now I want to ask you
something, Are you listening,
asshole, because I like you?
          (Racine nods)
I got a serious question for you.
What the fuck are you doing? This
is not shit for you to be messing
with. Are you ready to hear
something? See if this sounds
familiar. Anytime you try a decent
crime, there is fifty ways to fuck
up. If you think of twenty-five of
them you're a genius. And you're
no genius. You know who told me
that?

Racine remembers telling Teddy that.

                    TEDDY
Listen, man, maybe you should let
me do it for you. Gratis. I'll do
it. I wouldn't even be on the
street if it weren't for you.

Racine looks him over, shakes his head 'no.'

                    RACINE
Thanks.

                    TEDDY
I hope you know what you're doin'
you better be pretty damn sure
about it. If you ain't sure, don't
do it. Of course, that's my
recommendation anyway - don't do
it.
          (he puts a hand on
          Racine's shoulder)

>   Because I tell you, Counselor, this
>   arson, this is serious crime.

Racine looks at him.

INT. COUNTY JAIL - VISITING ROOM - DAY

Teddy Laursen sits across the table from Racine. Teddy,
too, looks a little ragged. Nervous.

>   TEDDY
>   I don't know. It's a thing in
>   Lauderdale. Something must've gone
>   wrong, but they're not telling me.
>   I'm a little worried.

>   RACINE
>   I'll find out.

>   TEDDY
>   No, no. That's not why I called
>   you. In fact, I got me another
>   lawyer.

Racine watches him.

>   TEDDY
>   I think it would be better. You
>   know Schlisgal.

>   RACINE
>   (nods, confused)
>   He's good.

Teddy looks around nervously. Racine waits.

>   TEDDY
>   This broad came to me last week. A
>   real looker. She said you told her
>   how to reach me, I figured you
>   musta, she knew all about it.
>   (Racine nods)
>   She said you wanted another one.

Teddy searches Racine's face, trying to see if the story was
true. He's not surprised that it's not.

                    TEDDY
          Yeah, I was afraid of that. But I'm
          a slow thinker.
                    (lowers his voice even
                    more)
          She had me show her how to rig it
          to a door, with a little delay.
          Does any of this mean anything to
          you?

Racine looks at him blankly.

                    TEDDY
          Then I'm glad I told you. Watch
          your step.

                    RACINE
          Thanks, Teddy.

Racine pushes his chair back. Teddy seems torn about saying
more. He forces himself to –

                    TEDDY
          Racine ... Don't thank me yet. These
          guys here, they've been asking me
          about The Breakers.
                    (reads Racine's look)
          I haven't told 'em shit. But I
          don't like the look on their faces.

Racine gets up.

21
PREPARING TEDDY

Carefully collect the facts about your character and challenge any assumptions you make. Give him a vividly imagined past and create some memories about key moments. Establish clear emotional states and objectives for each scene. Be wary of making decisions about past events that involve other characters until you can discuss them with the actors playing them.

Start with the facts

As you would for any other medium, you need to collect the facts about the character that are given to you by the writer. Start with what's objective and unarguable.

As is often the case in screenplays, there aren't many hard facts. Teddy is in his mid-twenties and an arsonist. He is able to rig an incendiary device quickly and easily. He has previously been in trouble with the law and what he says implies that he was represented by Racine and is grateful to him for what he did. The workshop in which the first scene takes place is Teddy's and he knows where everything is in it.

In the second scene, he is under arrest and has hired a different lawyer. He tells Racine that he has been questioned about The Breakers. He also tells him that a good-looking woman visited, claiming Racine had told her how to find him, and that he showed her how to rig an explosive device to a door.

Assumptions

As you read, you'll be making all sorts of assumptions and it's important to treat them with caution. You don't have the luxury of discovering in rehearsal that you're wrong and then having a leisurely rethink.

So be careful with any assumptions you make about events in the story. Read the whole script carefully and make absolutely sure you understand what's going on and what the dialogue means. If you make a mistake, it can really wrong-foot you on set when you realize your error. (It's also pretty alarming for a director to discover that an actor has misunderstood something in the script. At the time he may appear sympathetic and unconcerned, but internally he will very likely write you off as not very bright and no one wants to work with not very bright people. This may sound harsh, but under the pressure of shooting, it's what will happen.)

The other set of assumptions that need challenging relate to the character you're playing. So your next job is to work through these and use your intelligence and artistic imagination to distinguish between assumptions that are reasonable and appropriate and that do what the story needs and those that can trap you into making obvious choices: justifiable, but boring and hackneyed.

To do this you need to understand the function of Teddy in the story. He is there to supply two pieces of information to the hero. In the first scene, it's how to rig the fire at The Breakers. And in the second, it's to alert him to the fact that Matty plans to rig an explosive device to a door, something she has not told Racine. This generates suspicion about Matty in the minds of Racine and the audience and it is paid off at the end.

These two things must come through clearly because the flow of information through the story is incredibly important to the audience's involvement. That does not mean you must lean on it heavily. It's the director's job to make decisions about how much emphasis to place on things and he will give you direction if he thinks you are over or underplaying it. But whatever you create in your performance must not get in the way of this.

In addition to a compelling narrative, what makes any story interesting is the texture, detail and nuance with which it's told. That means if you are playing Teddy, we don't want to see a cipher delivering information. The director wants you to bring the character to life and he hired you to turn the words on the page into a real person, with a pulse and an inner life and you need to do some serious work to create this.

For example, it's a small step from the writer's description of Teddy to an archetypal low-life criminal: a rough-and-ready, chain-smoking biker, unshaven, tattooed, with drawling speech and unfortunate personal hygiene. Bad Hollywood films and television are heaving with this kind of stereotype, the hallmark of lazy writing and acting, and other cultures have their own yawning clichés.

My ambition for you is greater than this. It's not that such people do not exist, and it is possible that these external characteristics are precisely what the writer has in mind and the director wants to see because they offer the audience a shorthand. If so, you will need to invest heavily in making such a person real. Some of the characters played by Ryan Gosling could easily have been clichés, were it not for his depth of characterization and fierce commitment. For an example, look at his performance in *A Place Beyond the Pines*. But we all have an internal database of previously seen characterizations and it's all too easy simply to copy one of these, perhaps unintentionally. There may be much more interesting interpretations to explore and simply to stop at the first obvious choice is to waste an opportunity.

The other thing to mention here is that some of the things described in the script may change. You may not end up wearing jeans and a black T-shirt. Bruce Springsteen's music may turn out to be prohibitively expensive or the director may decide in post-production to use some entirely different type of music. There certainly won't be any music playing on set as you're filming.

The designer may persuade the director that Teddy's workshop is more visually interesting if he has a neatly organized and labelled storage system. You need to be prepared for the possibility that you will walk onto a set very different to the one you had imagined, in which case you will have to adapt and improvise, just as you will if another actor is doing something very different to what you had anticipated.

Aside from these external factors, you will also be making all sorts of assumptions about Teddy's history, character and inner life.

From Teddy's dialogue and what the writer tells us, it's reasonable to assume that he knows what he's doing when it comes to arson. But he might not. He could simply be an opportunist thief who set fire to a few things in the past, got a bit of a reputation and knows more about arson than anybody else Racine knows. It's your choice. To go too far with this line of interpretation would fly perversely in the face of Lawrence Kasdan's script, but it might be an interesting avenue to explore.

When Teddy tells Racine that he likes him and offers to do the job for him, I assume he is sincere. But he doesn't have to be. Teddy could be somebody with a strict moral code when it comes to paying debts and he offers to do the job for Racine hoping he will say no. It's your choice. If this is what you decide, then you must truthfully play Teddy's adherence to his moral code and this generates another question: Does he genuinely want Racine to believe in his offer or does he make the offer half-heartedly so that Racine will decline?

Your artistic choices will include the acceptance of some assumptions, the tweaking of some and, perhaps, the deliberate contradiction of others. An important part of your preparation is to recognize where you are making assumptions and challenge them to see if you can find something more interesting. The history of cinema is littered with landmark performances that played against the obvious and were huge hits. Think of Anthony Hopkins in *Silence of the Lambs*. The part of Hannibal Lecter could so easily have been another scowling, menacing psychotic killer: boring and obvious. Instead, Hopkins went the other way. Gentle, softly spoken, charismatic and charming, Lecter became the real star of the film.

Creating a past

I've already referred to the need to create real depth and complexity for your character. Doing this for the screen is no different to doing it for the stage, so whatever techniques you use to create characters will be valuable here, be it Stanislavski, Uta Hagen, some other teacher, a method approach or some system of your own devising. Again, be warned, one of the biggest obstacles is the absence of a formal rehearsal process and the input of a director and fellow actors. Finding the discipline to do this thoroughly, alone, is essential.

It's crucial for your character to have a vivid sense of personal history. You'll probably want to write yourself a biography, detailing where your character was born and grew up, what his parents do, how many siblings he has and so on. While it's important to do this, it can also be a little arbitrary unless you find ways of making it real for yourself. So, more important than the biographical facts you choose, is the work you do to create memories that feed into your character's engagement with the world.

In the case of Teddy, you might decide he had a middle-class upbringing against which he has deliberately rebelled and that he gets a kick out of the danger inherent in crime. If so, you might spend some time deeply imagining what he experienced when he first broke the law. Make up a backstory about this. Perhaps he had a friend at school, a year older than him, who was already a petty criminal, and Teddy went along for the ride on a shop break-in. Imagine the scene in detail and work through his experience. Picture what he saw. Try to create for yourself the feelings he had: the thrill when the friend first suggested it; the nervousness on the day; the regret about having agreed and the guilt when lying to his mother about where he was going; the nausea and fear as they approached the shop tinged with self-disgust at his own cowardice; the determination not to let himself down; the relief at realizing that his friend was also nervous; the excitement as they smashed the window and the rush of adrenaline as they entered the property. And so on.

The emotional experience of this is what will help you build a character. So work through the scenario you decide upon, blow by blow, imagining how it felt, searching for experiences of your own that have parallels and can help make the fictional memory real.

Do the same with other key moments on the road to Teddy becoming who he is now.

Perhaps, rather than the middle-class rebel, you might decide that he is the son of a drug-addicted mother, who never knew his father. Or that he comes from a family background in which crime is regarded as the family business.

Whatever backstory you give him, AVOID CLICHE. All the three scenarios I've outlined above contain elements of cliché so explore how you can twist them away from this. If he is a middle-class rebel, perhaps he later confided in his mother and was surprised to realize that, despite ostensibly disapproving, she secretly admired his wildness? In the second scenario, instead of never knowing his father, perhaps it was his mother who walked out and his father who raised him? Or, if he comes from a criminal background, perhaps his penchant for arson makes him the black sheep of the family? If so, why? Is this because it has the potential to hurt people? Because it's too risky? Or because it is viewed as a crime for cowards?

There are moments of character history that are crying out to be defined as memories and to be rooted in personal experience: the first moment he set fire to something and his feelings at watching it burn; his first encounter with the police; the first time he set a fire for money or advised someone on how to do it. There will surely be some parallel in your own life with the first time you experienced something thrilling. It doesn't have to be arson, of course; it's the feeling of exhilaration that's the point, not so much what prompted it. Your first time on stage? The moment you realized you wanted to be a professional actor? Your first pay packet as an actor?

Have you ever been arrested? If so, how did you react? Were you frightened? Defiant? Excited? If not, what's the most trouble you've been in with authority? Even if it's just being hauled in front of the head teacher at school, it gives you something to build on.

You're not trying to create an entire history that can be shoehorned into the subtext of a single line of dialogue. Rather, you are creating a real person with the complexity of past experience that we all have. Even if the audience doesn't explicitly identify this, it will infuse everything you do. And just occasionally, there may be a moment when it swims into focus. A great example of this occurs in *American Hustle* when Amy Adams' character, Sydney, gloats about her affair with the husband of Jennifer Lawrence's Rosalyn. The speed with which Rosalyn crumbles lays bare a lifetime's experience of rejection and self-loathing. In the hands of a lesser actress this could have been tiresomely superficial. But Lawrence's commitment and deep preparation turns it into something profoundly moving as we glimpse the ragged edges of her life story.

Make it relevant

Focus your attention on aspects of your character's personality that have a bearing on what he says and does in the scene.

Avoid creating some private, melodramatic or improbable personal history that has no bearing on what the character is required to do.

Spending your time concocting a complex series of memories relating to his first kiss with a cousin, aged 12, while on holiday in Wisconsin, won't help you portray Teddy Laursen any more convincingly. And it has the potential to introduce some off-note that will simply puzzle the audience if they get a sniff of it.

In the first scene Teddy expresses his concern for Racine and even offers to set the fire for him. In the second scene he tells Racine he has said nothing to the cops about The Breakers. Let's assume he is telling the truth, in which case you need a clear sense of his moral compass. This is probably not a phrase that Teddy would use and he might not even be able to define his own morality. But there will be things he is prepared to do, things he is not prepared to do and some fuzzy stuff in the middle that he might do under certain circumstances. His moral code compels him to make this offer to Racine, so you need to have some idea about his beliefs in terms of loyalty, friendship, risk, *honour among thieves* and so on.

Similarly, while it's perfectly feasible that Teddy has a plan in the second scene to ask Racine to lend him some money but the right moment doesn't present itself, for you to give Teddy this agenda for the scene would just pull focus. So your characterization and backstory has to be relevant to the scene and its role in the overall narrative.

Shared history

The shared history between your character and other characters within the scene needs care. In the case of Teddy, this means Racine. You cannot make decisions that are, effectively, binding on another actor. You *could*, for example, decide that Racine has represented you four times, including successfully arguing for a suspended sentence just 3 weeks ago, following which you went out and got drunk together. This is perfectly compatible with the line in the script *'I wouldn't even be on the street if it weren't for you'*.

However, the actor playing Racine may have devised a completely different shared history for you. He may have decided that he has only represented you once and that was 3 years ago, since when he hasn't seen you. What's more, he feels uncomfortable around you and doesn't fully trust you. Coming to you for advice is an indication of the risks he's willing to take to kill Edmund.

You must explore and take decisions about your character's own personal history and life experiences, because these are what make him who he is. But you cannot, and must not, commit yourself emotionally to past events involving other characters, if their playing something different would disrupt your performance or vice versa.

Instead, I'd advise you to talk to the actors playing the other parts at the earliest possible opportunity. Perhaps at the readthrough? If there isn't one, or you don't get to have the conversation, ring them and ask to talk. For some reason I don't fully understand – probably embarrassment – this rarely happens ahead of the shoot. But ask yourself how you would feel if you got a call from an actor playing opposite you, wanting to talk through your shared history. Almost certainly you would welcome it. Your agent will be able to get you the number of the production office. Ask for the production secretary and, depending on what phase of the production they are at, he may simply give you the other actor's number since they are all included on the cast and crew list. If this list has not yet been published he may need to ring the other actor and give him your number with a request that he call you. If you don't then hear from him, it's more likely that the actor chose not to ring you than that the production secretary failed to pass on the request. But even then, what have you lost through making the effort?

Similarly, if there is something important in your interpretation you want to talk over with the director, why not get in touch with him and pitch it to him? In all the years I was a director, I don't think I ever received a call from an actor wanting to talk over something in the part but, as long as it wasn't something trivial, I would have welcomed it. Just because most people don't do this doesn't mean you shouldn't. You don't become a great actor by doing what everyone else does. Especially if you have a characterization or an interpretation that plays against the obvious, why leave it till you are on set to get the director's response?

A couple of caveats about this. First, don't contact the director unless it's significant enough to warrant taking his precious time. There is a breed of high-maintenance, neurotic actor whose neediness is draining. Even if you don't come to regret having cast them, you quickly stop accommodating their requests on set.

And secondly, it's probably not wise to try to contact the star in this way. Most stars work hard and are very thorough in their preparation, but there is a pecking order and I'd advise you to respect it. You have to remember that stars are besieged by people wanting something from them, including the reflected glory of being their friend. So understandably they become wary and protective of their privacy.

Most stars also know what works for them in terms of methodology. A well-known British actor told me about being cast in a movie as an old friend of the lead character, who was being played by a major star. When they came to work together he expected that they would nail down the specifics of how long they had known each other, the circumstances under which they first met and worked together, etc. The star – an actor I admire – wasn't interested in doing this. For him it was enough simply to accept that they had known each other a long time and there was trust between them. The British actor sensibly went along with this.

What happened today?

Possibly the most important part of the past for your character is the immediate past. Just as in the theatre you must have a really strong sense of time and place and if you do not have this absolutely clear you will be exposed because the camera will see that your eyes are empty.

Where have you just come from? What were you doing 30 seconds ago? Define it and picture it. What were you doing 2 minutes ago? Ten minutes ago? An hour ago? And before that? What's been the most significant thing that has happened to you today? Did anything happen yesterday that is still reverberating for you? What's had the greatest impact on your current emotional state? (Again, make it relevant or it risks destabilizing the scene.)

For example if, half an hour before the second scene, Teddy was being interrogated by the cops who kept returning to the subject of the fire at The Breakers, then this will have a big impact on Teddy's exchange with Racine. The audience may not explicitly know about it, but they will pick up its impact on his emotional state.

So you need to create clear and specific memories for yourself about anything that is relevant to how you are in the scene. If, as Teddy, you were interrogated this morning, you need a strong, visceral sense of how this felt, not just an abstract, intellectual description of it in your brain. Improvise it. Lay out two chairs for two imaginary detectives on one side of a table and seat yourself on the other. Play out an increasingly fraught interrogation and commit yourself to it, answering questions and allowing yourself to feel increasingly pressurized. You're aiming to recreate the experience Teddy has had so that you can call on it just before you play the second scene with Racine.

Some actors use triggers to help them recapture particular states of mind. I can easily imagine, for example, that playing an arsonist like Teddy, you could decide that he has a small burn on one of his fingers which is still painful. Giving yourself a small burn (real or imagined) could help trigger your identification with your created memories and backstory.

What do you want?

We all have hopes and ambitions and fears and moment by moment this is what determines our behaviour. I'm deliberately going to avoid using terminology that relates specifically to any particular approach to acting, as there is often confusion between methods about words like 'action' and 'objective'. But the core ideas are ultimately the same and relate to being specific about a character's desires. Put simply: *What do you want?* Whenever we encounter a situation or another human being, we are striving to achieve something. We say and do things, not knowing how the world will react, but hoping for a particular outcome.

This has to be true for your character also. You must know very clearly what you want in the scene. Are you actively pursuing something in the encounter? Or are you benignly going about your day when another character forces their agenda on to yours, which causes a reaction in you?

Presumably, when Racine arrived to see him for the first scene, Teddy had no particular goal relating to Racine since he did not initiate the meeting. So his want is probably something simple like 'have a friendly chat' or 'help out my buddy Racine'. Racine's agenda is 'to acquire some knowledge'. By the time we join them, Teddy's want is to help Racine (i.e. to go along with Racine's agenda). But later in the scene a new want crops up for Teddy, as he becomes concerned for Racine's welfare and tries to change his mind about setting the fire.

In Teddy's second scene, however, he has a more active purpose before the scene even begins: he wants to warn Racine.

If you have trained, or are training, this will probably be very familiar to you. But without the prompt of structured rehearsal, it's all too easy to approach filming without having got this absolutely clear.

At the end of the process of preparation, you must take some decisions about who you are, how you feel about the other characters and what you bring into the scene in terms of history, emotional state, desires, etc. (though you need to be ready and able to adapt these to some degree if so directed).

But you should **not** take decisions about how you will actually *play* the scene. You must know what you want to achieve but without knowing how others are going to react. Just as in life, you will simply respond to what happens as you try to get what you want.

22
PREPARING THE TEXT

Learn the lines until they are absolutely secure. Rehearse them, out loud, exploring every interpretation you can imagine, including every possible way the other actors may interpret their lines. Investigate the scope for reacting. Don't commit yourself to anything or get too fond of any one interpretation. Your aim is to walk on set, absolutely prepared and ready for anything.

Learning the lines

My advice is to follow Michael Caine's dictum and learn the lines by rote, without any intonation, so they become like a reflex. Learn them so they are 100 per cent secure, so that if anyone reads a line from the script at random you know, without hesitation, what comes next. If you recite the alphabet, you don't have to think what comes after the letter 'E'. You just *know*. When you know your lines this well, all your attention can be focused on engaging with the drama and the other characters. Contrast this with what happens when you don't know the lines really, *really* well. At least some part of your inner monologue will be your own, not your character's, as you try to remember what the hell your next line is.

> Anthony Hopkins: *'I'm meticulous about learning the script. I always make sure I really know it, go over it and over it and over it until I feel comfortable with it. There's no strain, no "What do I say next?" I know it so well that I can just let it happen.'*

Without doubt there are some actors who are so intuitive and/or experienced that they are able simply to trust to the moment and an element of doubt about the lines enhances their performances. Instead of being an actor groping to find scripted words, they are able to hold on to the character and, by really listening, create a response in the moment, guided by the background work they have done on the lines.

But actors who successfully work intuitively this way are few and far between and since you are reading this book, I suspect you may not yet be one of these. In my experience, not knowing the lines is often disastrous for an actor accustomed to the luxury of theatre rehearsals and trying to make the transition from stage to screen.

Some actors talk about learning thoughts rather than lines. The danger with this approach is that until you get on set you usually have no idea how the other actors are going to play the scene or what the director is going to ask of you. So the scene, and your thoughts, may not follow the pattern you anticipated. Theatre rehearsals allow you to explore this and make collective decisions. But when filming, if you have learnt the scene by following a particular emotional pathway and this is challenged by what you meet on the day, you may find yourself lost. If, for example, you have learnt the scene on the assumption that there is sympathy between you and another character, only to find the actor playing that other character unexpectedly comes at it with hostility, you will have to adapt very quickly.

You should also brace yourself for the likelihood that there will be rewrites – usually minor tweaks – to the script as the shoot approaches or once it's begun. Once the shooting script has been issued, any pages of revisions – even a single changed word merits a revised page – will be issued on different colour paper so there's no doubt about the most up-to-date version. Make sure you replace the pages in your script with the new ones – you don't want to turn up on set having learnt an old version of the scene.

You just have to take rewrites in your stride and don't let the possibility stop you learning what you have as early as you get it. It's quite common for scenes to be deleted or added and, on occasion, characters to be cut entirely. If this happens to you, it feels awful. There will still be some sort of payment, but that can be cold comfort. The only consolation I can offer is that it's not a reflection on you.

> Hugh Bonneville: *'I'll familiarise myself with the week's work, study individual scenes the night before, then focus on the lines on the morning of the filming day itself. I aim to know them inside out but then try and forget that I know them, so they can take you by surprise. For me it helps with a degree of spontaneity.'*

Delivering the lines

In preparing the text your aim is to open up possibilities and doing so will probably form part of the process by which you define your character.

Learning the lines is only the start of preparing the text. Not committing to how you will say them does not mean you should not explore how you *could* say them. So once you have learnt the lines by rote, I suggest rehearsing the scene by yourself, trying to find as many different interpretations of it as possible.

There are two main purposes to theatre rehearsal: (1) your own exploration of your character, his situation, his intentions, how he behaves in pursuit of his goal and so on and (2) agreeing with your director and fellow actors the blocking and broadly how scenes will be played. The second of these will happen, usually at high speed, on set. So you need to do as much as you can of the first, on your own, beforehand.

Read your lines out loud, also reading the other characters' lines either silently or out loud. Personally, I used to find it broke my flow to speak the other person's lines aloud, but methodically reading them silently was an important part of my imaginative process. Whichever you do, you need to feel the rhythm and energy of the exchange. It's not enough simply to read the other characters' lines in a cursory fashion. It's a bit like the difference between scan-reading a passage of prose for its meaning and reading poetry, which is more kinaesthetic and requires you to formulate the texture and cadence of phrases in your mind, even if this happens silently.

What you are actually exploring is the exchange of **intentions** as characters try to influence each other. So you need to make the jump from a detached, intellectual appreciation of what's going on to a visceral, personal engagement with your own and others' intentions. You cannot really inhabit the character's life sitting at a desk, poring over a script and murmuring lines under your breath. So get out of your chair and physicalize the scene: aloud and moving.

Partly what you're looking to do is open yourself to the unexpected. Some of the best moments in things I have directed have been surprising, even counter-intuitive interpretations by actors. I have often approached shooting scenes knowing **exactly** how I wanted them played, only to watch an actor deliver an entirely unanticipated moment of inspiration which has opened up a whole expanse of meaning and nuance and subtext that neither I, nor the writer, had envisaged. Sometimes this was the result of spontaneous creation but often the way had been paved by the preparation the actor had done.

So don't accept your first interpretation. Try it again, differently. Try it the opposite way. Try it in direct contradiction of the obvious and the writer's intentions. Try it as many ways as you can possibly think of, without judging them to be right or wrong. See how many possibilities you can come up with that make emotional sense. And explore some that don't.

Parentheses

As you do this, don't get hung up on directions in brackets that indicate how the line should be delivered. They're just a guide. Shakespeare's plays have done well enough without directions to the actor on how to say the lines and he is liberating to work on. Liberation is what you're after as you rehearse.

There are two main reasons why writers put things in brackets in the first place. The first is to help the reader. Scripts are often selling-documents intended for financiers and executives, many of whom are speed-reading a lot of scripts and some of whom are either inexperienced and/or not very imaginative.

The second reason for using parentheses is to indicate to the actors how they should deliver the lines. Soap operas have a bracket for almost every line of dialogue, put there by the producers and the script department who are the guardians of the long-term storylines and who don't want actors interpreting lines other than the way they intend. If you were cynical, you might say they live in fear of an actor doing something creative.

If you're cast in one of these series – and they can be a good source of work – delivering the script as written is the job you have taken on. And while most of the regular cast will ignore what's in brackets, remember that they are dug in and hard to sack. If you're a guest actor, the rules are different. So while I'd encourage you to explore and go your own way, you do need to be prepared to revert to what's in the brackets on the day if you want to be asked back.

It's also important to understand that the director's job on these series is to deliver exactly what's in the script and he is under massive pressure to meet the schedule. Even if you have a valid artistic reason for your interpretation or a quibble with what's in the script, he is likely to get it in the neck if he changes anything. So do not make his job harder if you sense resistance to what you are doing.

(There is another, laudable school of thought that says you should **not** cooperate with the demands of mediocre or bad drama. David Mamet argues in his thought-provoking, compassionate, arrogant book *True or False* that actors should not desire the good opinion of fools and charlatans. While most script editors are not charlatans and only some of them are fools, I agree with him that it can be soul-destroying to participate in work that you know to be meretricious. But I also know what it's like to fret about paying the rent and to feel that work – any work – will help you improve and move on to better work.)

Further up the quality scale, your job is to be creative. So explore any interpretation suggested by the writer but explore alternatives as well.

This doesn't mean you are free to rewrite or paraphrase as you see fit, though it's legitimate to ask the director if you can alter a line slightly if you really believe it's an improvement. And of course, if the director is also the writer, you may find he has very fixed ideas about how he wants lines delivered. Directors differ hugely in how collaborative they are. Some, labouring under the delusion that the auteur theory is actually true, do indeed see actors as puppets. Others recognize that good actors bring enormous creative insight and are keen to take advantage of this.

What most directors do want, however, is an actor who brings a strong interpretation. Directing is exhausting, with people constantly asking you questions about absolutely everything. Bob Hoskins described it as like being pecked to death by a thousand pigeons. The job is much easier if people around you give you something to respond to, rather than expecting you to come up with everything yourself. So while actors absolutely need to be able to adapt quickly to any notes from the director, they also need to start from a point of view, with commitment, so he can clearly see what they're proposing.

Subtext and inter-text

There's an important distinction between the *subtext* – what the character wants the other person to understand – and what I shall call the *inter-text,* by which I mean the private thoughts that prompt him to speak and which drive both the choice of words and the subtext.

For example, consider the following exchange:

YOU
Can you lend me some money?

ME
Yes, of course.

If I don't want to lend you money, my inner response to your request might be *'oh no, not again. He's always doing this and never pays me back. I can't really get out of this so I'll have to say "yes", but if he sees that I'm reluctant, hopefully he won't press me on it'*. This inter-text will happen at lightning speed and I may not even be more than dimly conscious of these thoughts myself. But it determines my reply *'yes, of course'* which I will say in a way that deliberately makes my reluctance clear. The subtext – what I want you to understand – is the active communication, which might be *'I'm willing to but it's inconvenient and I'd prefer not to'*.

If, however, I don't want you to know about my reservations – perhaps, I want to keep in your good books for some other reason – the inter-text might be *'oh no, not again. He's always doing this and never pays me back. But I really want to keep him on side, so I'll act happy'*. I still say *'yes, of course',* but I do so with a cheery smile and a tone that carries the subtext *'I'm happy to help'*.

To help with the distinction I suggest using the second person – *'you'* – for the subtext, because it's about what I want to communicate to the other person. And the third person – *'he'*, *'she'* or *'they'* – for the inter-text because it's the inner monologue about the other person. Crucially the inter-text must lead to the impulse to speak the next line. As well as making for a richer, more coherent performance, it should also considerably ease the task of learning the lines.

No doubt the idea of subtext is familiar from your stage work. One of the joys of screen acting is that the camera's access to your inner world gives you scope to explore the inter-text, so it becomes much more important.

Subtext and inter-text in *Body Heat*

So you've done your character preparation and know what you bring into the scene as Teddy. Let us have a look at some of the lines in *Body Heat* to explore the subtext and inter-text. You'll get more out of this next section if you commit a bit of focused time to it – not long, perhaps half an hour – but it'll make more sense than if you dip in and out. It'll also help if you're familiar with the dialogue so either bookmark the pages of script, so you can flick backwards and forwards, or you might even want to learn the scene.

I'll start by assuming that you like and trust Racine and want to help him out, though there are alternatives, each of which will lead to a wholly different matrix of possible subtext and inter-text. And what I'll go through is only a fraction of the possibilities for this interpretation, but it should give you an idea of how extensively you can explore.

Even before Teddy's first line `whatsa matter, you can't think with a little music?'` he `'winces at the way Racine clips two wires together'`. You are not bound to wince just because the writer has put this. If you have decided that you don't like Racine and are ambivalent about helping him, then you might privately enjoy his discomfort.

But if we stick with the idea that you like him, perhaps you don't wince at all but instead smile fondly like an indulgent teacher with a favourite pupil. You then think to yourself (the inter-text) *'it's funny how this guy is so good with words, but lousy with his fingers. Look how rattled he is. And Bruce Springsteen is probably not helping him. He's probably more at home with that classical shit'*. This prompts you to say the line `whatsa matter, you can't think with a little music?'` with the teasing subtext *'Come on Racine, I thought you were smart'*.

Perhaps you notice a flicker of irritation on Racine's face and your inter-text continues *'he didn't like that. I like the guy, so I don't want to humiliate him. I'd better help.'* The next line `like this, I said'` is delivered more gently with the subtext *'sorry, I was just teasing'*.

Of course the inter-text *'look how rattled he is'* only works if you see that Racine *is* rattled. And *'he didn't like that'* only works if there is a flicker of irritation on his face. If, say, you see defiance on his face, the inter-text might be: *'He thinks he's smart? I'll show him that I know more than he does'*. Or if Racine is so intent on what he's doing that he doesn't seem to hear, the inter-text might be *'we are going to be here all day unless I step in'*.

There's also the possibility that Racine seems to be doing fine, in which case the inter-text might go *'he's doing okay for a beginner, but I want him to know what an expert I am'* and hence the intervention of `'Like this, I said'` with the subtext *'not bad, but see how a professional does it'*.

Or perhaps you feel slightly less indulgent towards Racine and take slightly more pleasure from your own expertise. Instead of *'he's probably more at home with that classical shit'*, the inter-text might be something more like *'he probably thinks rock "n" roll is just noise'*, so the line `whatsa matter, you can't think with a little music?'` becomes a little dig at Racine. You might still notice a flicker of irritation on Racine's face and it prompts a slightly superior `like this, I said` with the subtext *'you're no good at this, let me show you'*.

Returning to your stool you might be feeling satisfaction at Racine's appreciation of your expertise. Or you might be relieved that he has understood you. Or, perhaps you're baffled by how such a clever man can be so slow. There are many other emotions that might come up, and which you can explore by rehearsing, though you won't know what you actually feel until you get to the take and put your preparation together with input from the director, the other actors, the set or location and anything else that influences you as you look people in the eye, listen and tell the truth.

Depending on how Racine delivers his next line `that's it?` it might lead to some very subtle competition between you. If his tone suggests surprise at its simplicity – and his subtext to you is *'you made it sound complex but it's easy'* – then your inter-text might be *'he's getting cocky, is he? I'll remind him of the benefits of this. He asked for something simple and that's what I've given him'* before you embark on the speech `it's fast. It's hot...` delivered with authority.

Or maybe you don't detect anything critical in Racine and you pick up instead a concern to know that it really is that simple. Your inter-text is *'he's worried. He needs me to let him know that it really will work'*. So your lines `it's fast. It's hot...` have a subtext about reassurance *'hey, trust me. I know what I'm doing.'*

So you continue, through to the end, exploring branching possibilities of inter-text and subtext. At many, many points through the scene, even a tiny difference in intention from Racine will change your inter-text and send you somewhere else.

As I write this, it sounds a very dry process. You may find it valuable to go through this sitting at a desk, poring over the script, pencil in hand. For many actors this is an important part of preparation and they cover their script in notes. But for many others this is stifling. Whichever is true for you, it's essential to get on your feet and act it out. Imagine the scene and speak your words out loud. Imagine the other character speaking his, with all sorts of subtexts and see where they take you emotionally. *Feel* your way through the emotions at play. Practise connecting the lines to thoughts to emotions.

Remember that you're not looking to make decisions about how you will play the scene. Leave that to the take, when you will live in the moment. Right now you're just looking to explore how your Teddy might react to various possible Racines.

Sir Ben Kingsley compares the process to a racing driver walking the track the day before a race. He reads and works the scene on his own to establish what he anticipates is its overall intention, like a racing driver examining the tarmac, looking at the holes and the cracks, checking the bends, etc. on the course that he will drive the following day at an incredibly high speed.

Guard against becoming wedded to one particular interpretation. If you feel yourself falling into this trap, heed Olivier's advice about not using the 'right' inflection and force yourself to rehearse delivering it in numerous alternative ways.

And lastly, if you are one of those actors who deals with your anxiety about doing a good job by rehearsing it to death, recognize this and know that there is such a thing as over-rehearsing. Your aim is to explore the possibilities so that everything is flexible and supple but you MUST leave room for spontaneity and inspiration on the day.

Out there to *in here* and back again

It's easy to get hung up on the lines and how to speak them. But the words reflect only a small part of what is happening internally and what's really of interest to the screen audience is the whole of the character's experience.

As you prepare, look for moments when your character's inner monologue is particularly vivid. The camera loves these moments when your attention goes from *out there* to *in here* before going back *out there,* because they allow the audience a glimpse of your inner world, as long as you keep your eye movement within the doughnut. And if you can make them live, they are the moments when the editor will cut from the speaker to see how you react.

On stage the audience can only project onto the actors what they *may* be feeling or thinking during pauses so theatre directors are endlessly, and rightly, urging actors to pick up the cues. So taking time to allow thoughts and emotions to unfold can feel very indulgent to an experienced stage actor, especially one who is feeling the pressure of the shoot. But if you rush these moments they will pass for nothing, so do not be afraid to allow yourself the time to experience things fully.

This does **not** mean these moments of reaction need to be played long. The brain works incredibly fast, especially when responding to the unexpected or dealing with conflict, so even very complex thoughts and emotions can happen at lightning speed. And the audience is so very good at thin-slicing, you do not need to labour them. Trust that if you experience it, we will see it.

And you must absolutely avoid being indulgent. One of the toe-curling aspects of most soap operas is the way some actors overplay their reactions. And we have probably all worked with actors who are blindly convinced that the tiniest, most inconsequential hint of a thought that crosses their minds is of compelling interest to an audience. It isn't. It's simply egotism or an overwhelming need for attention and it's boring. Just as in the theatre, it's the screen director's job to tell you if you become indulgent, although he has far less time to notice this as his attention is on a hundred and one other things, and he may not notice until he sits in the cutting room and regrets having hired you. So if he tells you to speed things up, listen to him. But as long as they are filled and vivid and accessible, pauses while you digest what is happening are a vital part of the audience's journey through the story and they **will** hold our attention.

Teddy's second scene

Teddy's second scene offers three main opportunities for him to go from *not-knowing* to *knowing* as he understands what Racine is saying or doing, all marked by the writer.

The action-direction 'Teddy searches Racine's face, trying to see if the story was true. He's not surprised that it's not' confirms that Racine did not tell Matty how to find him.

With 'Racine looks at him blankly' Teddy further realizes that he may have inadvertently put Racine in danger.

And `(reads Racine's look)` removes any doubts that Racine rigged the fire at The Breakers.

All of these moments give scope for you to take a moment to absorb new information and consider its implications.

There are also many, many moments when Teddy might pause while speaking, as he considers what to say next and how to say it. In fact, pretty much every full stop offers this, often with further scope for it mid-sentence. But what you're looking for is moments where there is an interesting, *justifiable* internal thought process.

For me the most promising three are:

Before Teddy says `in fact, I got me another lawyer`. Perhaps he is embarrassed about not having turned to Racine? Perhaps he worries that it seems ungrateful? Or perhaps the police interest in The Breakers has convinced him that Racine is a dangerous person to be involved with. But all of them allow the possibility of his hesitating before breaking the news to Racine.

As marked by the writer: `Teddy looks around nervously. Racine waits.` He has something significant to tell Racine. Something about which he feels very uncomfortable.

And before `These guys here, they've been asking me about The Breakers` is a great opportunity to revisit, very briefly, the memory of just how intense the interrogation has been.

Any of these moments offers the potential for the kind of lateral eye movement I detailed earlier, as Teddy's attention shifts from *out there* to *in here* and back out to *out there*. And as you rehearse on your own, you can explore how these moments might work.

Lastly, the final moment of a scene often offers a great opportunity for your character to reflect. In this instance when Racine gets up, Teddy is left to ruminate on what's just happened. Stay in the scene until the director calls 'cut' and this might well be the last image of the scene in the cut.

23
MAPPING

You must know exactly where you are, physically and emotionally, at the start of every scene. To do this with larger parts you must create a timeline and map of what has happened previously in the story. Summarize the scenes, then identify exactly where you are and how you feel at the start of each.

Larger parts

Thus far, I've explored how to prepare for a part that has only one or two scenes. The likelihood is that this will be your early experience of working on screen. But how do things change if you are lucky enough to get a substantial part, with your character's own narrative journey, or even a lead, while still relatively inexperienced?

In many ways things become easier. You obviously have to put in the hours preparing the individual scenes but you've got more to go on when it comes to character preparation. And you'll probably find your nerves lessening as you get to know the crew and the shooting environment becomes more familiar.

But the one really significant and challenging difference is the need to know exactly where you are in that character's narrative.

It's imperative that you start every scene crystal clear about three things:

1   what has happened to you in the past
2   your emotional state
3   what you want from the circumstances of the scene.

If you have only one or two scenes, it's pretty easy to get clear on these before arriving on set. But if you have numerous scenes, you may have to be very organized to achieve this level of clarity.

In the theatre, once you have done the groundwork in rehearsal, it's relatively easy because the performance follows a linear path, moving chronologically through the timeline of the scenes. Even those very rare productions that move backwards and forwards in time still follow the same path every night. So once you've got it straight in your mind, it stays constant. But filming is done out of sequence, so you will almost inevitably shoot some scenes that occur later in the story before you've shot the earlier ones. And you may even find yourself shooting scenes that you don't know how to approach, because it will depend upon the undercurrent of earlier scenes that you haven't yet shot!

> Adrian Lester: *'At home, I rehearse myself and understand that flow through the piece. And then look at the shooting schedule, see what we are shooting at each point and know where my character was, physically and emotionally, at that point in the piece. So when that scene comes up I can think "I know what's happening now."'*

If you have more than one scene, it's vital to map your character's journey so even if you suddenly have to shoot a scene at short notice, you can reliably know exactly where you are in the story and what your character has experienced so as to locate the *'flow'* Adrian Lester describes.

For a spectacularly good example of mapping, watch Tahar Rahim as the protagonist Malik in the French film *A Prophet*. Malik's narrative arc is epic as he evolves from vulnerable innocent to brutal and ruthless crime boss. Rahim's compelling performance is beautifully nuanced and his clarity about where in the journey Malik is, in any given scene, is astonishingly secure.

I'll use the character of Ned Racine to show how you can create such a map. As I write, the screenplay of *Body Heat* is easily available online, so I would encourage you to read it.

Summarize the scenes

To start with, make a list of all the scenes in which you appear, summarizing them with a sentence describing what happens to or for your character and, in particular, whether he moves towards or away from something of importance to him.

The first four scenes of *Body Heat* are all expositional as Racine watches a burning building as a girlfriend gets dressed, gets criticized by a judge in court for his poor quality work, banters with his lawyer friend, Lowenstein, and then meets another client, a rich, old lady. With the exception of Lowenstein, none of the characters will reappear but the scenes establish Racine's character and the world of the story.

In the fifth scene, the story proper kicks off as Racine successfully chats up a beautiful, married woman, Matty. She initially plays hard to get but then encourages his attention. Having spilt ice cream on her dress, she sends him to fetch a paper towel. When he returns, she's gone.

So in this scene he takes a significant step towards something he badly wants: intense sexual excitement. (This is perhaps not great news if you're playing the girl in the first scene: your job is to be available, but unexciting. On a more serious note, understanding your casting can be crushing. Even more so than in the theatre because it's less to do with your acting range and more to do with what you *are,* or at least how you seem.)

A sequence of very brief scenes then underlines Racine's boredom as he jogs, works and screws around.

Next he tracks Matty down in a bar in the wealthy suburb where she lives. When she agrees to let him come back to her house, he takes another significant step forwards. But, concerned about her reputation, she slaps him and publicly tells him to leave her alone. He exits, uncertain about whether her anger was genuine or a cover. Sure enough, in the next scene she drives home, allowing him to follow her.

So a one-sentence summary of these opening scenes might look like this:

- Racine watches The Seawater Inn burning as his date gets dressed
- a judge criticizes Racine's work
- Racine banters with his friend Lowenstein
- Racine charms an elderly female client
- Racine meets Matty and establishes a connection with her before she runs out on him
- Racine jogs
- Racine listens to a divorcing couple argue in his office
- Racine drives past Pinehaven Yacht club
- Racine watches as a nurse, another conquest, gets out of his bed and dresses
- Racine finds Matty in the Pinehaven Yacht club bar. She agrees to let him come back to her house, but then slaps him. He walks out
- Racine follows Matty's car back to her house

Asking the right questions

For each of these scenes, you need to be able to locate yourself and know exactly where you are, physically and emotionally, in your character life. So part of your preparation is to know the answers to the questions that will allow you to do this.

So for the first scene, among other things, you need to know:

- Who is the girl?
- When and how did you meet her?
- Where is your apartment?

- What did you do this evening?
- How often have you slept with her?
- How do you feel about her?
- How do you feel about your life generally? Are you content?

To play the second scene, you need to know:

- Who is your client and what, precisely, is he accused of? (This may involve some research.)
- What do you think and feel about your client? Do you think he is guilty? Do you care what happens to him?
- How well do you know Lowenstein and how do you feel about him?
- What do you think and feel about Judge Costanza? How often have you faced him?
- What condition is your lawyer's practice in? Do you have lots of clients and cases? Or are you in need of work?
- How do you feel about your work in general? Is it rewarding? Boring? Challenging? Mundane?
- How do you feel about your life, both personally and professionally?

You get the idea. While it may not matter too much if your decisions about some of the more tangible elements – the wheres, whens, whats – are slightly arbitrary, it's particularly important to know how you *feel* about the other characters. You – the actor reading this book – could describe your feelings about people in your life and these feelings will hugely influence your behaviour towards them. Similarly, how your character feels about the other characters will ripple through your playing of the scene.

Once the story proper is under way your awareness about what has happened previously, both on screen and off, needs to be very precise. In particular, you need to be very clear about the passage of time. Shooting scripts – the published scripts used for pre-production – will assign the time of day, but this is primarily to help departments like lighting and design. The script you use for the bulk of your preparation probably won't give the time of day and the number of days between scenes almost certainly won't be specific.

Some of the early scenes in *Body Heat* are almost continuous – there is a time jump of probably less than an hour between the second and third scenes. And even less between Matty slapping Racine in the bar and his following her in his car. Some involve a longer, non-specific time jump, for example, between Matty running out on Racine after spilling ice cream on her dress and his finding her in the bar. There is an implication that it has taken him some time and effort to track her down, but whether this took days or weeks is unclear. Added to which, the passage of time can be emotional more than literal for a character caught up in a story. Forty eight hours to a man in the throes of what will become a murderous infatuation, can feel like weeks.

So if you are playing Racine, it is incredibly important that you go into the scene with a very precise knowledge of how long has passed since you met Matty, how many places you have looked for her, how you feel about her, how often you have thought about your initial meeting and so on.

If you are playing Matty, it is similarly important to know how long has passed, what has happened for you, whether you have seen your husband, whether or not you have had sex with him, how many other men have tried to chat you up and how and why (and even whether) you have rejected them.

Obviously the length of time that has passed is something that needs to be agreed between the two actors, and perhaps the director, but the decisions about what you've done, thought and felt, especially about Racine and your husband, are yours alone to take. Since, as we later discover, Matty has been planning murder from the very beginning, part of her need at this stage is to test the lengths to which Racine will go in pursuit of sexual gratification. If he's not willing to put in heroic effort to pursue her, he's not going to succumb to the level of erotic fixation necessary to kill her husband, which is what she ultimately wants from him.

By the time Teddy puts in an appearance, Racine is committed to his plan to kill Matty's husband, Edmund. The scenes immediately prior to this might be summarized like this:

- Racine bumps into Matty and Edmund at a restaurant. Edmund invites him to join them

- Edmund tells Racine a little about himself and Racine feels both challenged and inadequate

- Racine watches Matty through her bedroom window

- While out running, Racine sees The Breakers, a derelict wooden hotel on the seafront that Edmund and his associates own

- Racine tells Matty they are going to kill her husband. She agrees

- Matty insists on accompanying Racine as he visits Teddy, though she agrees to wait outside

- Teddy shows Racine how to set a fire

So when you come to shoot the first scene with Teddy, you need to be absolutely clear about the timeline leading to this. How much time you have spent with Matty recently? How long it is since you first met her? How long has passed since you suggested killing her husband? How does the relationship with her compare with other relationships you have had? Specifically, since sex is a driving force in Racine's motivation, how does the sex compare? You need to know Racine's recent history as well as you – the person reading this – know your own. And your mapping needs to allow you to pinpoint this with emotional accuracy.

The inner life of your character will sometimes be influenced by things in the story that are happening off screen either right now or in the near future – for example, a getaway driver approached by a policeman while his accomplices are holding up a bank or stopped for speeding on the way to meet his bank robber accomplices. So your mapping needs to include all relevant events and characters that are off screen.

Even if you would do this work naturally as part of your theatre preparations, you need to have it in a reliable and easily accessible format, so you never, ever shoot a scene without absolute clarity. And the bigger the part, the more complex it becomes. There's no standard way of doing this but the following example offers you a possible mapping template for Racine for the first scene with Teddy.

Question	Answer
What am I doing as the scene starts?	I'm trying to put together the incendiary device Teddy just showed me.
What's my emotional state as the scene starts?	I'm concentrating hard. I'm a little embarrassed. It looked easy when he did it, but I can't seem to get the wires to cooperate.
	I feel a mixture of nervousness and excitement about being here. I also feel a little rattled, that I've already crossed a line simply by asking Teddy about this. And the music's too loud to let me concentrate.
What was happening 30 seconds ago?	Teddy was explaining how to rig the incendiary device. I understood it at the time, but it looked fiddly. It reminded me of physics lessons at school, which I never really liked. I had to remind myself to pay attention while he was explaining it.
What has happened in the last 5 minutes?	I left Matty in her car round the corner from here. I had to put my foot down to dissuade her from accompanying me. I don't want her implicated any more than she has to be and Teddy would only be distracted by her presence.
	I rang the doorbell twice, but got no response and had to knock loudly and shout. I knew he was in, because I could hear music. Having to shout made me nervous, because it drew attention to me. I don't think I was seen by anyone else but I don't want there to be any witnesses to my having come to see Teddy.
	After a few pleasantries, I explained to Teddy that I needed to know how to set fire to something. Thankfully he didn't ask any questions about why. He explained briefly how the device works and did it once for me to watch. But it was quick and I didn't see clearly what was involved.

(Continued)

Question	Answer
What has happened in the last hour?	Matty and I made love in her and Edmund's bed. I wouldn't admit it to anybody else, but I got a thrill from the knowledge that I was fucking the wife of that man – whose power and wealth make me feel inadequate and whom I am going to kill – in his own bed.
	I told her I needed to go to see someone who could help me with the plan to kill Edmund. She wanted to know all about it. Initially I refused to tell her and we came close to an argument before, eventually, I explained how we will put his body in one of the derelict buildings in The Breakers and set fire to it so it looks like it was done by his business associates.
	Part of me wants to protect her by not telling her the details. But part of me wants to share the burden with her and have her admire my planning.
	She drove me to the docks so I could show her the building. On the way there I told her I know a professional arsonist who can show me how to set the fire. She quizzed me about how I know him, whether I trust him and so on. She insisted on accompanying me and said she wanted to come in to meet him so we share the risk. She was really forceful. I haven't seen her like this before.
What's the most significant thing that has happened in the last 24 hours?	I told Matty what I have known for several days: that we are going to kill Edmund. She hadn't said it but I know that she's been imagining it too, ever since she told me that she wishes he'd die. She consented, happy to be led by me.
What happened in the last scripted scene?	Twenty minutes ago I tried to persuade Matty that I should go to visit Teddy alone because I don't want her implicated any more than she has to be. While she agreed to stay in the car, she insisted she wants to take the risks with me.

(Continued)

Question	Answer
What has happened since the last scene?	Matty drove us from the harbour and parked around the corner from Teddy's workshop. As she drove, I tried again to persuade her that she should not come with me, but she insisted. It's a rundown neighbourhood and I felt uncomfortable leaving a beautiful woman alone in an expensive car, so I told her to lock the doors. But I knew there was no point in saying anything more and I also know that she is very capable of taking care of herself.
What's happening off screen right now, or in the near future, that is relevant to me?	Matty is waiting in the car outside for me. We are going to kill her husband so we can be together and enjoy his money.
What else of significance has happened recently?	It's 5 weeks since I started seeing Matty. I've felt more alive in those 5 weeks than I have felt for years.
	It's 3 days since that evening in the restaurant when I met Edmund. That's when the idea of killing him occurred to me seriously. I'd thought about it before this, but only in an abstract, detached way, not as a real possibility. At first I thought I haven't got what it takes to kill another person, but ironically, it was Edmund himself who convinced me that I have. The way he talked down to me and all that smug bullshit about being willing to do what's necessary. And then the way he talked about Matty, as though she is just another possession. I want his life. I want his wife. And I'm going to have them.
	I couldn't sleep that night, imagining him with Matty, his hands all over her, and his self-satisfied face leering at her. And by the morning I knew we're going to kill him. I needed a couple of days before telling Matty to get used to the idea and to come up with a plan. But then when she came to my office like that, I knew I had to tell her because we have to be very, very careful from now on.

(Continued)

Question	Answer
How do I feel about Teddy?	I like him. I know I shouldn't approve of him or what he does. But I get a thrill from the way he lives his life and, in some ways, I wish I were able to live with risk like him. Well, I'm about to take the mother of all risks and it feels exhilarating.
	I also trust Teddy. I've acted for him three times. The first time was when a pimp I've defended, Steve Jarvis, recommended me. Jarvis is a nasty piece of work so I was wary of Teddy at first, but when he told me he also dislikes Jarvis, I warmed to him. I was going through a quiet period professionally so I needed the work and arson seemed like a step up from defending pimps. I got him off. The second time I acted for him, he got a suspended sentence. The third time was when he called me in a panic. Having been unable to get hold of me, he'd appointed another lawyer, Goodman, who had told him to plead guilty. Before the case came to court, Teddy had changed his mind, after talking to some other prisoners, who had told him he could get 5 years. But Goodman was resisting changing the plea. When I went down there, I saw immediately that the police had not followed proper procedure. After a bit of an argument with Goodman, I took over the case, argued the procedural point with the judge and got Teddy off. He was touchingly grateful. And so he should have been. Without my intervention he would have spent at least 2 years in jail. One of the reasons he was looking at a 5-year sentence was because he had refused, point-blank, to grass on anyone. So I feel pretty confident that he is trustworthy and that asking his advice on how to set a fire is safe.

Once you map all the scenes there will be lots of repetition but this can help create the certainty you need. I'm also not attempting here to find Racine's voice, as I'd recommend you do for any character you're playing.

It's worth going into some things in further detail, for example, the timeline of your acquaintance with Teddy, what he had been charged with and so on. And clearly there are things that you would need to run past the other actors and be flexible enough to change if need be.

A note also about managing your own invention. Let's assume you have not met the actor playing Teddy. Even if he's an actor whose work you know, you don't know how he's going to play the part. So you can't afford to commit yourself to things that may not be there in his characterization. For example, your preparation and mapping might include *'there is a straightforwardness about him'*. But you don't know that there will be a straightforwardness about the Teddy you're confronted with on set.

Even what I've written about his being trustworthy is slightly dangerous. What do you do if you get on set and are confronted with someone who is patently untrustworthy? In your preparation you're trying to balance the need to make your relationship with a character you've never met real and specific without committing yourself to things that may be unsustainable.

Your own understanding of Racine and how to play him will develop through the shoot, as will those of the other major characters, especially Matty. So as the characters develop, along with your working relationships with the other actors, you will probably need to go back to rework elements of your preparation. At the very least you will probably find yourself making tweaks to it. And you may have to go back and change your mapping, as things emerge when you film scenes. For example, regardless of which scene with Teddy is shot first, you may need to rework your mapping before you play the other scene. All this is normal and necessary.

24
THE READTHROUGH

Most productions, apart from soaps, will have a readthrough, attended by the whole cast (if they're available), director, producer, writer, script editor, executive producers and any heads of department – design, costume, Director of Photography, production manager, 1st AD, etc. – who have been appointed. It's everyone's first opportunity to hear the dialogue from the mouths of those who'll be playing the parts. If it's a series, you'll probably read the first couple of episodes.

There are many similarities with a theatre readthrough, although it's more important because it's likely to be the only time you'll ever all get together and, following it, you'll do the rest of your preparation alone.

You'll probably be nervous. So will everyone else. It's the beginning of whatever relationships you'll forge during the production and a chance to gauge what it's going to be like to work on. You'll also get a sense of the director, producer and other key people in the production process.

Prepare well for it. Since you may not receive the script until a day or two beforehand, I'd advise you to keep some empty space in your diary for this.

You're not aiming to deliver a definitive performance but giving an interpretation of the part as you plan to play it will (a) be helpful to the key creative people, (b) allow those playing opposite you to get to sense of your characterization and (c) allow you to get a sense of the dynamic between your character and the others.

It's also an important opportunity to establish relationships and initiate a dialogue with the actors you'll be playing opposite, whom you should seek out. Get there in good time and don't arrange any appointments immediately afterwards. It can be tempting to think you look cool if you have other things to dash off to. Looking cool is nowhere near as useful as going for coffee afterwards with the person who'll be playing your spouse or lover.

25
AT THE SHOOT

What to expect from being picked up to your arrival at the location or studio and the run up to shooting the scene. There will be lots of waiting around but you must make sure you are absolutely mentally prepared when you are called to set.

Getting there

Depending on the size of the budget, you will either be contacted by the 2nd AD about your pick-up time – good news, they're sending a car to collect you – or be told what time you need to get yourself to the production base.

Generally speaking, in the United Kingdom at least, it's only the long-form TV series (those that are in production all year round) and low-budget films that require you to get yourself to the production base. It's not that the others have money to waste, but the disruption to the schedule (and the financial consequences) caused by an actor failing to show up when he's required, mean that they'd rather pay for a driver to make sure you get there on time. Because long-form TV series have a rolling schedule, in the event of an actor not turning up or arriving impossibly late, the scene can be slotted in on another day. This will make you hugely unpopular of course, but it can be done. And unless some scenes with the actor have already been shot, the part can, if necessary, be recast. Low-budget films simply don't have the money and are in an almost permanent state of improvisation around production difficulties.

The perception among the usually efficient people who work in production is that actors are flakier than non-actors. I don't know whether this is true but do not contribute to it, for the sake of all actors and your own career. Do not be seduced by the many stories of wacky, unreliable star actors. At all points in the casting process, up to and including the major Hollywood stars, the reasonable, personable and reliable actor will always get the job in preference to an equal talent who is hard work. It's unarguable that some stars bring a certain magic that means a little bad behaviour is sometimes, *sometimes* worth tolerating. But, believe me, if another star with equal magic and who is easy to work with is available and interested, they will always get the gig. And a star who gets a reputation for being awkward finds his career in free fall once his name on a poster no longer guarantees an audience.

The call sheet

A call sheet is issued by the 2nd towards the end of every day for the following day's shoot. This details all the logistical and practical arrangements, including the schedule, locations, phone numbers, any special equipment or effects and so on. It will also list the names of the actors, their characters and their travel arrangements including times of pick-ups, arrival at production base, wardrobe, make-up/hair, travel and arrival on set.

The call sheet is usually physically handed to you, on paper, before you leave the set, if you are shooting the next day. If you are not present the day before you shoot, it will probably be emailed, or possibly hand delivered, to you towards the end of the day. Check it carefully. If there are any discrepancies or there is anything you don't understand ring the 2nd and ask.

If, for some good reason, you need to be picked up from somewhere other than your home or the hotel where they're putting you up, talk to the 2nd as early as possible. He will usually do his best to accommodate this, especially if he has a few days' notice. But bear in mind that the logistics of a shoot are enormously complex and to rearrange a pick-up, especially at the last minute, means extra work. So don't create a problem for the poor, stressed, sleep-deprived 2nd unnecessarily.

If anything crops up that has the potential to prevent your being present for the pick-up, it is absolutely imperative that you let the 2nd know immediately. So if you:

- injure yourself and spend the night in Accident and Emergency
- decide to spend the night at your girl/boyfriend's or your parents' *(my advice – don't, unless you've discussed it with the* 2nd *several days ahead)*
- go out and get drunk the night before a shoot *(my advice – don't, unless you are deeply, deeply committed to method acting and playing just one scene in which you are hung-over. And even then my advice would be* 'don't') and wake up in a strange bed

LET THE 2nd KNOW AS SOON AS POSSIBLE. His number is on the call sheet and, if you have more than one day's shooting, put it in your phone memory. There are a few hours in the middle of the night, probably midnight to 5.00 a.m., when he would rather you didn't call because there's nothing he can do about it. Either side of these hours, he would prefer to know sooner rather than later because then he can make emergency arrangements.

On the day, be ready when the car arrives. In fact, be ready before your pick-up time. Do not sabotage your own performance by not being ready. If you are responsible for making your own way to the location NEVER, EVER BE LATE. It puts the fear of God into everyone and establishes you as 'trouble'. Even if you are charming to everyone, you are still 'trouble' and this is not going to be good for your career. Being late doesn't make you bohemian/interesting/creative. You either are or are not those things already. It just means that, in addition to either being or not being bohemian/interesting/creative, you are also late. So if you are travelling by public transport, leave time to get the bus or train before the one you need, in case it is delayed.

A standard shooting day is 8.00 a.m. to 7.00 p.m. If you're in the first scene of the day, you will probably be into make-up and costume somewhere between 6.30 a.m. and 7.00 a.m., depending on how complex your hair and make-up are and how many other actors they have to prepare. So this may well involve a pick-up between 5.00 a.m. and 6.00 a.m.

Arriving at the set or location

If you're shooting in a studio, you'll have a dressing room. If you're on location, you'll have a trailer. Depending on the budget and the size of your role, you may be sharing with another actor. But either way, you will have somewhere quiet and private to prepare.

You will probably be there long before you are needed. Pick-up times allow for traffic problems. Call times are deliberately arranged with slack in them so there will probably be quite a lot of waiting around. This is not just people being careless with your time. The ADs are all working to ensure maximum efficiency of shooting. They want to know that they can deliver you to the set, as required, regardless of whether someone spilt coffee over your costume or your make-up took longer than expected or the director shoots a scene unexpectedly quickly and gets to your scene 45 minutes early.

It's worth saying that there is a huge amount of unseen work by the AD department going on to make the shoot run smoothly. They are constantly tracking people and equipment to make sure everything and everybody is where and when they are needed so that shooting is never delayed. Generally these people are hugely professional and they deserve your respect and cooperation. On the rare occasions when you run into someone less than sympathetic, rise above it. Not only is it better for your karma, but your performance is unlikely to be improved by getting drawn into petty conflicts.

Depending on the production, you may be expected to get yourself to make-up and costume at the right time or there may be runners who come to fetch you. Do not leave it to the 3rd AD or the runners to get you there on time. Be professional and take responsibility for being ready when you're needed. (Having said that, have the conversation with the 3rd /runner about whether you should wait to be told to go to make-up. It creates a lot of extra work and anxiety for him if he has to chase round the location searching for an actor who has helpfully taken himself off to make-up but failed to tell anyone).

Your scene partner(s)

Depending on the nature of the scene, any hiatus between your arrival and being called to set is a good time to talk to any other actor(s) who'll be in the scene with you. In fact this is another good reason to be glad your call is usually early.

At the very least you'll probably want to introduce yourself, unless you have a good reason for wanting to meet them for the first time on set. Even if you are a deeply committed method actor about to play a scene with a character who's unknown to your character, it's usually advisable to have met the person you'll be working with before you begin rehearsing because, at the end of the day, you're still a couple of actors who have to play a scene together.

Beyond this, it's a negotiation between the two of you. You may happily find you both want to do the same thing in terms of preparation, be it just chat or run the lines or discuss how you are going to play the scene or rehearse. Or you may find you want totally different things – perhaps one of you is desperate to rehearse while the other is very keen **not** to rehearse, so as to keep things spontaneous. At this point you are simply two professionals figuring out how you'll work together, balancing collaboration with integrity. You may be happy to go along with what the other person wants to do or vice versa. The pecking order of experience may come into play, as will the relative size of your parts. And by 'negotiation' I don't mean to imply conflict. Usually you find some sort of easy compromise. But anything that involves compromise is, at heart, a negotiation. Be gracious and generous where you can, to create the goodwill that will allow you to hold out for things that are important. But equally, you should not allow yourself to be railroaded into things that will harm your performance.

As you know by now, my suggestion is that you agree a shared history of what has happened before the scene begins (where it involves both of you) but not make decisions about how the scene will play – leave that to the moment of the take. But many actors want to rehearse and you must find your own approach. Whatever you do, make sure it's deliberate, rather than simply going along with whatever's easiest.

Things are slightly different if you are in a scene with the star. Basically, what the star says, goes. Just as in the theatre, but even more so because you're unlikely to meet them at all, other than on set. Most actors are actually pretty generous-hearted and the reaction of the star described by Hugh Bonneville in his foreword was unfortunate, but not the norm. Nevertheless you do need to understand and accept your place in the pecking order because a reputation for upsetting stars will not help you get work.

What you also have to remember about the star is that he will probably have scenes with many other characters in the course of the story. So while the relationship with him may be very important for you, his character's relationship with you may not be so significant to him. He will be focusing his attention on the major relationships in the story and, if that doesn't include you, he may be less enthusiastic.

Waiting, waiting, waiting

No doubt you'll have heard about how much time on a shoot is spent waiting around. It can be surprisingly easy to lose track of time and not be ready when you are needed. This is an important part of being professional. When I used to play the triangle in the school orchestra, it usually involved counting endless bars of silence and then coming in with a single note. The skill wasn't really in hitting the triangle with the stick. It was in the counting. If you messed this up, you played the note in the wrong place. Hopefully your contribution is a little more creative and significant than my triangle playing, but you do need to be in the right place at the right time. And while others are there to help you, you are being paid to do this, so make sure you do it right.

It can also feel surprisingly lonely. Hanging out with other actors is usually one of the joys of theatre. If you've ever done a one-person show, or a two-hander, you'll know how quiet and subdued it can feel.

The make-up and costume rooms or wagons are usually light and hospitable. You sit in a comfortable chair and friendly, warm people fuss over you and make you look good. You're feeling the excited side of nervous and this is just about the most glamorous part of filming. You then go back to your dressing room or trailer and it's all lonely again.

There may be other actors around, of course, or you may be sharing a trailer or dressing room. Sometimes this is reassuring and enjoyable as you discover mutual acquaintances, compare notes on jobs you've done, who you've worked with, where you trained, etc. But sometimes you're on your own or the other actor doesn't want to talk. Whatever situation you find yourself in, you are at work, and what you do in the run-up to being called to set will hugely affect your performance.

Preparing yourself

Take seriously the work of being ready. Warm up. Obviously. You'll have your own physical and vocal warm-up techniques from your theatre work.

You'll probably be nervous. Recognize that nerves are good but they do need managing and that there are constructive and destructive ways of doing this. I mentioned elsewhere that one of my habitual ways of dealing with nerves is to be late. This does not help me deliver my best work. Your job is to be brilliant when the director says *'action'*. So find a way to manage your nerves that enables you to walk on to set utterly prepared and ready to be brilliant.

It's all made more difficult by the fact that you do not know exactly when you will be called. This lack of certainty can be very unsettling for a theatre actor used to the fixed timeline of *'the half'* through to *'beginners'*.

The call sheet will have an approximate time for your scene(s), but this will almost certainly change, frequently meaning you shoot later than planned. It's a standard 1st AD joke that, regardless of budget, it's an epic movie in the morning and a fast-turnaround soap opera in the afternoon. Most directors get caught up in their own ambition to make something beautiful and spend too long on the scenes in the first half of the day, so have to make up the time in the afternoon by shooting very quickly. This means that if you're in a scene towards the end of the day, it's much more likely to feel rushed.

If you don't get to your scene until after 6.00 p.m., brace yourself: it's likely to be very hurried. I worked on one soap opera where an actor referred good-naturedly to the '10 to 7' slot. This was the last shot of the day and it had to be done in 10 minutes flat. He knew exactly where to stand on the set, because this was the easiest place to light and shoot. He could have been difficult about it, grumbling and unhappy and stressed. But instead he was good-humoured and helpful and consequently was a terrific asset to the show. Not only did he help the shoot run more smoothly, but his easy-going acceptance of the budgetary reality meant that he could focus his attention on his performance and deliver the best that could be achieved under the circumstances.

You will probably be given a warning 10–15 minutes before you'll be called to set, so you can get yourself ready. It's worth checking with the 3rd /runner what the practice is on the production and requesting advance warning if need be. If you haven't done a warm-up do it now (though I'd strongly suggest you don't leave it this late). But even if you have, there's a lot to be said for warming up again at this point, not least in that the activity will put your adrenaline to use and calm your nerves.

Because the camera is so much more searching in its scrutiny, very few actors can rely solely on performance technique, the way some do in theatre, bantering in the wings before walking onto the stage and giving barnstorming performances. So you need to be emotionally engaged in the character's world and dilemmas when you walk on set.

What do you need to do to get yourself in the right frame of mind while you're waiting to be called? Do you need to sit quietly on your own and meditate? Or run the lines to ensure they're secure? Can you ignite something in yourself by focusing on certain past experiences? Will a low-energy activity, like doing the crossword or reading the paper, distract you in a way that will help your performance? Or do you need to find people to chat to about inconsequential things? None of these are the right or wrong things to do – it depends on whether they put you in the right headspace. My advice is to avoid conversations that go beyond the superficial or things that take you deeper into a world that is not your character's, like answering emails or reading other scripts or novels. But whatever you do, do it because it will help you deliver.

Phones

For this reason, and several others, do not take your smartphone onto the set. You will be tempted to check it for texts, emails, football scores and so on, and this will mentally take you away from the job in hand.

There is also the more immediate reason that your phone making any sort of noise whatsoever is an absolute sin on a film set. Just imagine how you would feel if you gave a deeply vulnerable, gut-wrenching performance only to have somebody's phone go off during the take and have to reshoot it. You may tell yourself you will turn off your phone between takes, but it is just too easy to forget.

You may see members of the crew using their phones. For some this may be part of the job: texting colleagues, checking emails that relate to equipment or the logistics of the shoot and so on. But even if they decide to run the risk of using it for personal reasons, most of them are on set all day, every day and have devised a foolproof system for making sure their phone never disturbs anyone else's work. They also do not face the same challenge that you do of being exposed, on camera, by even the slightest hint of a loss of concentration.

(As you may already have discovered, phones that are on 'silent' but still vibrate are not silent at all. So if, against my advice, you decide to take your phone onto the set and don't switch it off, make sure vibration, as well as the ring tone is turned off.)

26
WHO'S WHO IN THE CREW

The people in the crew with whom you will work most are the camera operator, boom operator, 1st AD and 3rd AD, art director, stand-by prop master, make-up artists and wardrobe assistants. Try to establish good relationships with them; they can make your life much easier and vice versa.

Who do you need to know in the crew?

Generally speaking, members of a film crew are friendly, just like most people are friendly to their colleagues at work. What follows is a brief glossary of the key people that you will interact with the most and with whom you need to make friends:

Director of Photography (DoP) a.k.a. lighting cameraman

He is responsible for all aspects of the photography. The DoP frequently also operates the camera but if there is a separate camera operator, the DoP will focus his attention on the lighting, which is a huge part of the look of the film. In fact, getting the lighting right is usually the longest part of setting up a shot so the DoP will generally be having continual behind-the-camera conversations with the camera operator and director about the look and with the 1st AD about timing. His work will have a huge bearing on how *you* look. He may occasionally ask you to find a light, in much the same way as it can happen on stage, but beyond this the DoP role doesn't require that much interaction with actors on set, although they spend a lot of time staring at you. (And the role is so significant that they are usually leaders within the group dynamics of the crew.)

Camera operator

He is responsible for composing the shots and is the person on the crew with whom you will work most closely. He will frequently ask you to adjust your positioning on the set to help his framing. He will direct the placing of your marks and will often need you to look at another actor while he checks eyelines. Cultivate a good relationship with the camera operator because he can make your life much easier and you can do the same for him. If you're one of those actors who likes to know the shot size, the operator is the person to ask. He will almost invariably also be a talented photographer in his own right. If the DoP is operating, his concentration will be split between lighting and composition so you'll have less of his attention.

Focus puller

He works closely with the camera operator to make sure everything is in focus. It's a highly skilled job and you will often find him measuring the distance between you and the lens by holding a tape measure by your face. Most go about this sensitively but you can make his life a lot easier by cooperating.

Boom operator

It's incredible that nearly a century after the first 'talkie', the actors' voices are still mostly recorded by someone holding a microphone on a stick – the boom. Capturing the sound is usually a two-person job with the actual recordist sitting round the back of the set somewhere with a trolley full of equipment. The more gregarious half of this team is the one holding the boom. The sound would be best recorded by having the microphone about 6 inches in front of your mouth and the boom operator's job is to get it as close as possible to this without it being visible in the shot.

You can tell roughly how wide the shot is from where the boom is. On a wide shot the boom will be several feet above you. On a close-up, it will be just a few inches above your head and will move to stay as close as possible to the mask of your face. In a dialogue the boom may swing backwards and forwards to capture both voices. So a microphone, possibly encased in a fluffy windsock, will be moving about distractingly close to your face. Get used to this and be friendly to the boom operator – he's only doing his job and most do it as discretely as possible. Occasionally you may come across one who simply doesn't seem to understand how off-putting it is for an actor. If it gets really bad, have a quiet word with the 1st who will, in turn, have a quiet word with the boom operator.

1st Assistant Director (1st AD, more commonly known as 'the 1st')

Confusingly, the 1st is not an assistant to the director. If the director is lucky enough to have an assistant, he will be known as the director's assistant. Rather, the 1st is head of the Assistant Director's department, which has the responsibility for organizing all the logistics and mechanics of the shoot on set. The 1st himself runs the set, a bit like a sergeant major, keeping everything moving, chivvying people along, lightening the mood or cracking the whip as necessary. If you have any concerns while on set, other than to do with the acting or other actors, he is the person you should talk to. It's an incredibly difficult job. The great majority of them are well-intentioned and understand how important the performances are and how difficult it can be for actors. The 1st is also the boss of the 2nd and 3rds and if the unit fails to meet the schedule, it is usually the 1st who gets fired, whether or not it's his fault. Having said this, any scheduling questions should be addressed to the 2nd AD, not the 1st.

2nd AD (or 'the 2nd')

He is responsible for getting everyone to the right place at the right time. He prepares the call sheet and will make sure you get into wardrobe and make-up in good time, organize your trailer and, most importantly, have you taken or escorted to the set.

If you have any problems to do with scheduling, talk to the 2nd, though be aware that he is juggling many things and cannot be expected to arrange shooting around your dental appointment or to accommodate the fact that your oldest friend has just flown into town. What is taken seriously, however, is other work commitments. Most ADs are also freelance, so they understand the need to juggle work. If you're lucky enough to have more than one job and they overlap, the 1st and the 2nd usually pull out all the stops to facilitate this. It's not unusual for the 2nds on two shoots to liaise with each other about who will have which actor when.

3rd AD (or 'the 3rd')

The 3rd is the 1st's right-hand man on set. He will have specific duties including things like briefing and organizing extras also known as back-ground artists or walk-ons. 3rds are almost invariably friendly and help-ful, floating between on and off set, and this is whom you should talk to about any minor problems. It will often be the 3rd who comes to get you from your trailer and who will tell you when your role in the scene is fin-ished or you can go to lunch. Never EVER leave the set without checking first with the 3rd (or the 1st, if the 3rd is off the set). It is absolutely infuriat-ing for everybody on the production to be waiting for an actor who has wandered off to the toilet or to make a phone call at the wrong moment. And the 5 minutes spent looking for you may cost the director a crucial shot later in the day or cause the whole production to go into overtime.

Runners

Runners are the next step down from the 3rd and, as the title sug-gests, do everything and anything they are asked. So it may be a runner who comes to get you from your trailer or who offers to get you a cup of tea or coffee. They are generally (though not always) inexperienced and trying to get their foot in the door of the industry, so are keen to get on with everybody. They usually have no authority whatsoever. By this I don't mean don't bother to be nice to them, but don't expect them to know what is going on in the big picture, what time you will be finished or to give you permission to do anything.

There may also occasionally be runners working for other depart-ments, for example, art or camera. They are there to help that department, and again, as individuals, they are trying to get their foot in the door. So do not expect them to be able to assist you.

Art director

He is responsible for the execution of the set design and the look of everything within the frame, including spotting objects that shouldn't be there, for example, lamp stands, cables, etc. A significant part of his role is the placing and continuity of props so do not play with them between takes. And even if you think you're being helpful by repositioning props, you're not. The art director will usually be a borderline obsessive–compulsive perfectionist, you're unlikely to position it in just the way that he would do it, so he'll re-position it when you're not looking.

Stand-by props

Art department assistants with particular responsibility for providing and maintaining on-set props. There are usually a couple of these guys who double as handymen/carpenters when anything in the set needs fixing.

Script supervisor

He (I'll stick with this convention even though the script supervisor is usually a woman) has a variety of jobs to do with keeping notes and preparing records for the editor. He is also responsible for continuity. I deal elsewhere with the importance of this but if you have any questions about what you did in previous takes, the script supervisor is the person to ask. He is usually to be found sitting by the director's monitor. Most of them are highly skilled at noting down physical action within the take, even if several characters are in the frame. Having said that, he may not be able to tell you absolutely everything you did. He may well approach you after a take to correct your continuity or if you are getting a line wrong. If you dry completely during a take, he may prompt you, but only if you ask for it, as he will never want to take the risk of crashing in on your meaningful pause.

If you want to paraphrase a sentence of the script, or change a word, it is sometimes worth asking the script supervisor, rather than the director if he is busy. They often function as the director's adviser and confidante and may be able to judge whether it's sufficiently important to bother him with.

Wardrobe

The costume designer, or wardrobe supervisor, will originally fit your costume(s). Assistants will maintain and check them when you first get dressed each day. On-set wardrobe assistants will check them again before each take.

Make-up

The make-up designer, or senior assistant will do your initial make-up at the start of your day. On-set make-up artists will touch it up during final checks. They're usually employed on a daily basis so may come and go through the shoot.

Other people you may occasionally interact with

Camera assistant – third rung down in the camera department.

Grip – responsible for camera positioning and movement. He sets up the tripods, lays track and manages any camera movement during a take, including pushing the dolly. A more skilled job than most people realize.

Gaffer – the chief electrician. Works closely with the DoP.

Sparks – the electricians. They work to the gaffer.

Sound recordist – may very occasionally ask you to alter your volume though it's usually the boom operator who relays this request to you.

Stunt coordinators and performers.

Visual effects supervisors – these people are responsible for rigging and managing any effects that are seen in the shot like fires, explosions, objects falling over, etc.

Caterers – food varies from terrific to not-so-good, but an army marches on its stomach and producers know that a well-fed crew works more efficiently than a hungry one. Food is free, except for on long-running series with a studio base, which will usually have a permanent canteen where you pay cash.

27
THE PROCESS
OF SHOOTING

On set

Finally, the moment arrives when you are called to set.

Two big shocks await the novice screen actor. The first is the sheer size of the crew. Dozens of people are involved in filming and the overwhelming majority of them are not actors. So it can be quite intimidating walking on to a set where all these people are milling about, doing their jobs, apparently friends with each other but uninterested in you, the lowly actor. In fact most crews are reasonably friendly but they are busy with their own roles and won't have time to welcome you. You need to carry a strong sense of self.

The second is the almost total absence of rehearsal time. They're pretty much isn't any, at least not in the way there is in theatre. You turn up on set, probably having encountered your fellow actors as you passed through make-up or collected a coffee, and quite possibly not having seen the director since the casting. You block the scene, rehearse it a couple of times and shoot it. It's not unknown for two actors playing a love scene to arrive on set, shake hands as they meet for the first time, take their clothes off and get into bed.

The sequence of events will usually be as follows:

(1) *Clear the set*
The crew leaves, with only the director and the script supervisor remaining, although often the 1st AD and the Director of Photography (DoP)

will also stay and watch. If time is tight, as it often is, other people may also be invited to stay and watch the rehearsal, for example, the camera and boom operators. They are not trying to interfere and certainly will not comment while you block and rehearse. They are simply trying to get ahead and will be silently planning. However, their very presence can inhibit your ability to rehearse and experiment freely.

(2) *Block*

Usually the director will tell you what blocking he wants. How precise this is will vary from director to director and sometimes from scene to scene. It may range from very precise instructions like *'you start by the cooker, turn and walk to the window on this line, turn back to say this, then cross to the table and sit down'* to loose suggestions like *'why don't you start by the cooker? Then, at some point, cross to the window'.* Remember he is managing the hugely complex machinery of shooting and will have had to make decisions beforehand about equipment, coverage, how the scene will cut together with the scenes before and after it, how long he has to shoot and so on. Therefore he will probably have a detailed plan of what shots he wants and your job is to slot into this and make it work.

Very occasionally you may find yourself working for a director who gives the actors a totally free hand to go wherever they like with no initial guidance: *'Show me what you want to do'.* Oddly, this can be quite destabilizing: too much choice with not enough time to work through the options.

(3) *Rehearse*

You run through the scene a few times, feeling your way through the character's actions and objectives. The director may amend one or two things. You or the other actor(s) may make suggestions. There may be some brief discussion about subtext.

It's worth being clear about the purpose of this initial rehearsal: it's primarily to agree a shape for the scene and establish the physical movements that will dictate how the scene is shot. It's not like a conventional theatre rehearsal, where you hammer out precisely what is taking place between the characters, all the nuance of relationship, subtext, inter-text and experiment with delivery of lines until you feel you have got things right. You'll do some of this between rehearsal and the take and some of it you won't rehearse at all.

(4) *Show*
The rest of the crew is then called in and you show the scene, as blocked, so that everyone can see what the action is: who moves where, what props are involved and so on. Each department will watch to see what it involves for them. Be clear about this: no one is watching for the drama, so do not expect applause or appreciation of your performance.

(5) *Coverage*
The director, DoP, camera operator, grip, art director, boom operator and 1st will then talk through the coverage, making decisions about how it will be lit and shot, where the track will be laid, how the boom will get in and so on.

Quite often you will be asked to run through the scene again, stopping and starting, so the camera operator can line up his shot and initial marks can be put down.

(6) *Set up the shot*
The various departments set to work while you and the other actors either go off to make-up or wardrobe or to your dressing room or trailer to relax. Or sometimes you'll be asked to stay on set if the operator needs you for line-ups. On big budget productions there may even be a couple of stand-ins whose job is to do this for you, though the days of stand-ins in UK television are pretty much over.

(7) *Camera rehearsal*
When the first shot is ready you'll be called back to the set and there will be a camera rehearsal. This is primarily for the technicians – the camera and boom operators, grip, perhaps the art department or visual effects – to practise what they will do during the take, so again you may be asked to repeat actions.

(8) *The take*
When everyone and everything is ready, the 1st will call for *'final checks'* – the opportunity for on-set costume and make-up assistants

to make a last check on clothes, hair and make-up. He will then call for quiet, echoed by the 3rd AD. Everyone goes still and silent and the instruction *'turnover'* or *'roll camera'* is given. The camera operator and boom operators will reply *'speed'* or *'rolling'* to indicate that they are recording. Then either the 1st or the director will call *'action'*, sometimes preceded by *'stand by'* or *'and . . .'* which is a sort of *'here it comes'*.

28
REHEARSAL

Rehearsal is about blocking, lighting and lining up the shot rather than defining what will happen emotionally between the characters. You are likely to be called upon to adjust your motivation to make the shot work.

The purpose of rehearsal

In essence, a theatre rehearsal allows actors to find their characters and establish a robust way of staging the scenes that can be repeated, night after night, so that every audience has a similar experience and sees a polished and well-constructed piece of drama. By opening night therefore, everything will have been fairly thoroughly rehearsed. It may not always feel like this but, believe me, compared with filming it has been rehearsed to death: the actors will have done their experimenting and know pretty much how they're going to play the scenes.

The reason there is very little rehearsal in filming is not just due to the mechanics taking priority. The intense scrutiny of the camera means that spontaneity is paramount, as you try to get as far away as possible from repetition or reproduction and, in many ways, rehearsal actually damages the performance.

So being ready does not mean knowing precisely what you're going to do. The whole process of preparation and rehearsal is about being ready to commit yourself to living truthfully in the imaginary circumstances.

Juliet Stevenson: *'A take is a mixture of planning and spontaneity. I love being surprised in a take.'*

You will have explored possibilities beforehand as part of your personal preparation. You may well run the lines with your fellow actors in your trailer earlier in the day. You'll rehearse briefly with the director before showing to the rest of the crew and there are moments of rehearsal for the technicians during which you are also rehearsing. Then you, as your character, need to be in a state of suspended animation at the start of the scene, knowing absolutely who you are, where you've come from and what you want, but with no idea of what's going to happen next. Just like you do in reality as you go about your daily life.

Of course you, the actor, do know broadly what's going to happen because you've read the script. You'll know the major physical moves and what's required of you technically to make the shot work. But what you won't necessarily know is what's going to take place between you and the other characters emotionally, what subtext you'll hear or how you'll deliver your own lines. This you'll discover afresh on every take as you react spontaneously to what happens during the scene.

To return to Sir Ben Kingsley's metaphor, you simply hit the ball back across the net, however it comes at you.

Hugh Bonneville: *'In a theatre play you have to nail it night after night and that's what the two or twelve weeks of rehearsal is for, so that you can begin to build a sense of what the rhythm of the scene is. After repetition and exploration, you gradually find a way of doing it and then you share that with an audience, without it being too ossified. But if you treat arriving on a film set like an opening night, you're in danger of ossifying straight away because you're not living and breathing with the other actors. You have to treat each rehearsal of a scene and then each take of a camera angle as if it's the entire rehearsal process and tech and preview rolled into one so it's constantly alive.'*

There is usually, however, scope to snatch moments of rehearsal while the shot is being set up. Wherever you are between 'showing' and the first take, take responsibility to rehearse what you need to rehearse, including any physical actions. In particular, if you have to hit a mark, work out how you're going to do this – paces or peripheral vision – and practise it so you are 100 per cent reliable by the time of the camera rehearsal.

The other significant player is the director. Most likely you will have no real idea of what he is looking for beyond the fact that he cast *you*. There may have been one or two clues along the way to turning up on set: your costume, the readthrough (if there was one). But you must be absolutely ready for the fact that he may have a very specific idea about how he wants you to play the part and you may have to abandon what you have prepared, in an instant, and commit yourself wholeheartedly to his alternative.

Don't lose sight of the fact, though, that you are not simply a mannequin. You are an artist, bringing a unique creative interpretation to the part, and that is why you were hired. Actors frequently find things in a role that neither the writer nor the director had seen and the best continually surprise you with the unexpected. What all directors want from actors is originality and insight coupled with a user-friendly professionalism. But most would sacrifice a little user-friendliness for inspiration.

So there is a balance to be struck between being responsive and collaborative on the one hand and overly biddable on the other. Shooting is full of negotiation and compromise. Low-level and hopefully amicable: a professional collaboration between colleagues rather than a tense exchange of *'I'll do that if you'll do this'*. Think of a theatre rehearsal when you ask another actor to change the way he does something in order to give you a better prompt for one of your lines. In return, you're happy to reciprocate when asked: it's give and take. Occasionally, if what the other actor is suggesting interferes with what you are playing, you push back and, hopefully, reach a compromise you can both live with. Very occasionally you may find yourself working with an actor who is so selfish it's all take and no give. No one wants to work with this person.

The give and take is pretty much the dynamic between you and the technicians on set, except that you are likely to hear many more non-negotiable moments of *'I need you to do this'*.

Making the blocking work

A good director will be reluctant to force an actor into moves he doesn't believe in. But it is also an essential part of the actor's job to find a way to make the blocking work and that means creative flexibility with your own motivation. The real reason you are making some physical move or raising your volume (rare, but it happens) may be to *make the shot work*. But your job is to do this while still living truthfully in the imaginary circumstances, so you must invent a motivation to make it work.

A good example might be the way that two people walking, side by side, as they converse can suddenly stop, by unspoken mutual consent, continue the conversation face to face, before then resuming walking. We all do it and we're dimly aware that both stopping and setting off again don't happen at random but are prompted by what's passing between us. It might be that one person stops because they experience an *in-here* moment, perhaps surprise or resistance or delight. Or perhaps one person has an *out-there* reason to turn to the other: to press a point, to seek advice, to deny, to thank or something else that involves reaching out to the other person.

Let's say you arrive on set to play Teddy's second scene and the director has decided to play the scene as you walk down a prison corridor. He wants you to stop part way through the dialogue so Racine can turn 180° to face back at you. He might be happy for you to figure out between you when this happens as long as he gets his shots. Or he might have a technical reason for wanting you to stop on a particular line and your job is to find a compelling inner reason to do so.

Your movement is a physicalization of the inner monologue so I'll look at how you could motivate the required stop on various different lines – the inter-text – and the subtext that might emerge from it. In this example I'll assume that you like Racine but the cops have been leaning on you heavily: you're frightened as well as wanting to warn Racine.

After Racine's line `'I'll find out.'`
Inter-text: *NO! I don't want him getting involved. Right now the cops are so interested in Racine that if he starts sniffing around the Lauderdale case everything will get worse for both of us.*

Subtext: *'Thanks but that's not a good idea.'*

After `'No, no. That's not why I called you.'`
Inter-text: *He thinks I'm after another favour. I need to break it to him about the woman but first I've got to tell him I've asked Schlisgal to represent me.*
Subtext: *'Look, I've got a confession to make.'*

Before `'This broad came to see me last week.'`
Inter-text: *Time to bite the bullet and tell him I may have dropped him in it.*
Subtext: *'There's something else I need to tell you. Something much more serious.'*

And so on.

In the first example, stopping is primarily motivated by the inter-text – internal thoughts about Racine as a third party – and in the other two by subtext – implied communication with him. But any given point in the dialogue can provide the motivation to stop. And similarly, you need to motivate the decision to start walking again.

I'm not suggesting you plot this in advance – after all you didn't even know you were going to be walking until you got on set – but you MUST find a motivation for the character to deliver the move that's needed. If, as you stop, your inner monologue is the actor's *'I have to stop here because the director wants me to,'* then this is what we'll see in your eyes.

This doesn't necessarily all need to be worked out instantly in the few passes before you show the scene to the crew. The initial rehearsal is simply to establish the rough positions so the crew can start setting up the shot. You may want to grab any rehearsal you can, with the other actor, on the fly, while this is going on as you figure it out.

Whenever coordinated physical precision is required from actors, my advice is to work out exactly who will do what and when. This may seem to contradict what I've said about spontaneity but uncertainty about the blocking creates hesitation in the actor and can seriously detract from the scene. This applies especially to sex and fight scenes when embarrassment or fear can easily prey on the actor's mind and coordinating it like a dance move actually frees you up to commit to the imaginary circumstances.

In some shots your physical positioning can be easily amended if you find a better motivation for a move. But in some it can't because a very specific place has been lit and dressed. So if you decide you want to change from what was shown to the crew TELL THE 1st AD IMMEDIATELY. If he's left the set for some reason, the 3rd AD will be on set so tell him and if you can't see either, tell the camera and boom operators. They will be able to advise on whether it can be done.

If the physical positions can't be changed, you may be able to make it work by walking a little faster/slower and getting to the required position a little earlier/later in the dialogue. If not, or your partner doesn't want to play ball, you may have to stick with what was rehearsed. If this is the case, you will need to use any spare time to find a truthful reason for the blocking and rehearse any moves so you can reliably hit your mark.

Camera rehearsal

Despite being primarily for the technicians to rehearse their moves, the camera rehearsal also gives you an opportunity for a final rehearsal. And don't be shy about asking for an opportunity to rehearse any specific physical moves if you need to. Everyone would rather afford you a few seconds to do this than have to do repeated takes because you messed things up.

In terms of playing the emotional content of the scene and how you'll deliver the dialogue, you are expected to be ready for this without further rehearsal. Having said that, if you really need another rehearsal, ask for it. But recognize that there simply isn't time for you to go over things again and again as you would in theatre.

29
THE TAKE

The mechanics of filming can seem to dominate proceedings but you must not be put off by the quantity of technicians who hugely outnumber the actors. If you stumble you must recover and stay in the scene until you hear *'cut'*. The director, via the camera, is the eye of the audience. Your job is to be brilliant on *'action'* so concentration, managing your energy through a long, stop-start day and generating your own mood are essential skills.

Surrounded by people but all alone

Most of the process of filming is orchestrated around the technical requirements of making the shot work and, for much of the time, relatively little attention is paid to the performances. So you may sometimes have to fight the feeling that you're simply a walking prop. The take is your moment: remind yourself that the actors are the most important element of most shots. The audience relates to people, not lighting states or props, and without strong, convincing characters, truthfully pursuing their desires, the story will fall flat.

In describing the differences between the stage and screen, I've stressed the need on screen to live truthfully and described the level of commitment required to create the imaginary world without the support of the audience's collective imagination.

But there is something additional about a film set that requires you to be much more focused and self-reliant than in the theatre. There will be upwards of 30 people doing jobs that are vital but many of which have the potential to break your concentration. What's more, many of them are watching you during a take. This can feel, to a stage actor, very much like an audience that needs to be pleased. It isn't and it's important to realize that they're not looking at you at all. Rather they're looking at whichever aspect of their own craft is reflected in you – the light on your face, whether your hair looks right, which way your head will be turned as you speak, etc. It requires a lot of concentration to filter out this attention, and focus on your character's wants and actions, without getting seduced into 'showing' acting.

The 30 seconds before 'action'

Possibly the single most important part of your preparation is what you do in the 30 seconds before the take. You must have deep inner clarity about where you (the character) are, what you want and how you feel, including how you feel about the other characters. In this, it's exactly like the seconds before you walk on stage. You need to be both physically and vocally warmed up and mentally relaxed so you can commit yourself absolutely to the fictional reality.

Great screen actors know exactly how to compose themselves, finding the right emotional state. Many have some sort of ritual, whether it's a visible warm-up or a private internal process for focusing their attention. One of the pitfalls for inexperienced actors is a failure to manage these seconds well. They succumb to the temptation to think they can simply turn it on when 'action' is called. Unless you are truly exceptional, you can't, and the camera will expose even the tiniest gap in your emotional commitment.

Your job is to be brilliant

Your job is to be brilliant when the director calls 'action'. It is not to move furniture or carry things for people. If there are props to be repositioned, that's someone else's job, not yours. I've seen many inexperienced actors trying to help out members of the crew. Well-intentioned, but misguided. And I say this not to be precious or to defend some anachronistic job demarcation. It's about you doing what you are paid to do as well as you possibly can. And anything, *anything* that gets in the way of it damages your performance and, ultimately, the drama.

Helping you to be brilliant is partly why they send a car to pick you up, why people in make-up and wardrobe pamper you and why runners may bring you cups of coffee. There's an unspoken recognition that the actor, unlike anybody else in the crew, has to be absolutely in the right mindset to work. Don't abuse this luxury treatment. But accept it for what it is and play your part in delivering flawless concentration when it counts: between *'action'* and *'cut'*.

It is a universal etiquette of filming that no one should make a sound or move within an actor's eyeline during a take. Whenever there is movement it will inevitably break the spell. Your concentration, even if only for a split second, will be disrupted and the camera will see it. Stage actors are used to audiences who cough and shift in their seats and occasionally unwrap sweets and they often pride themselves on their ability to rise above it. But the theatre audience is too far away to see the flicker of disruption it causes and this 'macho' approach doesn't hold up under the camera's merciless scrutiny.

Christian Bale got a lot of criticism for his rant, a few years ago, at a Director of Photography (DoP) who walked on to set in the middle of a take to check the lighting. But it seems to me that he was entirely justified. *'Do you understand my mind is not in the scene when you are doing that?'* yelled Bale. Well, no, it wouldn't be. Given that Bale was playing a character under extreme pressure, it's perhaps not surprising he expressed it the way he did. But whatever you think of his behaviour, the real villain of the piece was the DoP.

Hopefully you will never be confronted with such insensitivity on set. Those people whose jobs have the potential to distract you – the boom operator and the grip for example – will work with maximum discretion and you are entirely justified in asking for anyone else in your eyeline to be still and silent during a take. Some actors ask for their eyeline to be entirely clear of anyone who doesn't need to be there. Though I'd suggest you ask politely for any adjustments: the ranting thing is really only an option for major stars.

Recovering

Even if you dry or fluff a line or something else goes wrong you must recover and get back into the scene. Only the director calls *'cut'*, unless someone is hurt or in danger, in which case the 1st AD, who has responsibility for health and safety, will do so. There may be all sorts of reasons why the director wants to continue with a scene that may seem to you to be hopelessly lost. He may, for example, be happy with a previous take apart from one moment where, say, the focus was off or the boom came into shot. So he's running the scene to capture this moment but doesn't want to embarrass the person responsible by publicly announcing the reason.

Continue the scene until you hear the director call *'cut'*. Never, *ever* stop before this, even once the dialogue and any action has finished. Stay in character, stay in the scene and continue to live truthfully in the imaginary circumstances. Do not allow your thoughts to stray to the question *'when is he going to call "cut?"'* The dialogue finishing is actually a fantastic opportunity for you to explore internally what has just taken place and many of the best moments happen when words have run out and characters are either left staring at each other or alone with their thoughts.

You should never look directly at the camera unless you are explicitly told to do so by the director. A surprising number of actors are frightened of doing just this and their fear causes them either to avoid looking anywhere near the camera or, weirdly, to look straight down the lens. There is no way of consoling you if you do the latter: you just must not do it. On some subconscious level you may think that if you're quick enough, we won't notice. But we will. We always see when an actor looks at the camera, no matter how briefly, and that moment is unusable.

Take two

Once the director calls *'cut'*, he will either announce that he's happy and the 1st will move the crew on to the next set-up or you will go again, in which case there may be an extended hiatus while various changes are made to improve things. This can take as long as half an hour and you will probably be hanging around on set throughout. In exceptional cases it might even take longer if the entire shot gets rethought and the 1st or the 3rd may suggest you return to your dressing room or trailer.

If the director has no notes for you, this means he's happy with what you're doing, so accept it as praise by default and don't go looking for him to verbalize it: he has many, many things on his plate and can do without insecure actors demanding attention.

If he does give you notes, it can feel as if the need for another take is all down to your failure. Whereas, in fact there may be other, unseen reasons – something to do with the pictures or sound – and since he has the opportunity, there's a detail in your performance he wants to tweak.

There are many elements to a shot and getting them all to come together in a single take is difficult. So brace yourself for the fact that the take where you really nail it may have a problem in another department and you'll have to do it again.

Tim Robbins: *'You have to roll with it. You can't let things upset you. If there is a plane that comes by in the best take you have ever done as an actor, it's not going to be used, so you have to just let it go and come back to it when there is silence.'*

Whether there'll be lots of takes or only a few, depends on the schedule, the budget and the shooting style of the director. Some like to turn over as soon as possible and then do numerous retakes, adjusting things as they go. Others like to get everything right before the first take, so there are very few retakes.

When everybody is ready to go again, the 1st calls for quiet, the camera rolls and you live in the character's world again. While you need to repeat your physical continuity, trying to recreate what happened emotionally in a previous take is likely to result in something contrived. Each new take needs to be approached as if it were the first one.

> Sir Ben Kingsley: *'In filming each take is a creation and you simply respond to what comes at you from the other actor. It would be no good an actor complaining to the director that the other actor did not say that line the same way in the other take.'*

As the takes clock up, it's easy for an actor to become convinced that it's all about his failure. At which point he tenses up and goes into a downward spiral. If this happens, mentally shouting at yourself won't help. Calmly bring yourself back to your character's inner world and what he wants.

> Adrian Lester: *'If there's any tension, the camera will pick it up, and it will say straightaway* "I don't believe you because I can see you trying, and trying is effort, and if you have to make an effort, it's not real." *'*

Working with the director

Clearly one of the biggest differences between acting on stage and screen is the physical absence of an audience. The stage actor continually monitors the audience response and makes very subtle changes to his performance. The most obvious example is riding a laugh. No point in coming in with a next line if the audience is still in hysterics at the previous one.

The screen actor doesn't get this feedback. But what he does have is the director. In theatre, the director's job more or less comes to an end on the opening night, when he hands over the production to the actors. Of course he gives notes and he, or an assistant, will attempt to keep the production on track through the run. But, performance by performance, things evolve. Sometimes the actors discover greater depth. Sometimes the audience response subtly reshapes things. And sometimes, let's face it, the production gets infested with cheap laughs. But, essentially, the director ceases to be involved once the audience arrives.

The screen director, by contrast, is almost totally in control of the audience experience. He decides which takes get used and can dramatically change your performance through his editing choices.

For the screen actor, he **is** the audience so listen to him. This is not simply a question of trying to please him because of his power. He is the only person who can offer you the kind of feedback you would get from a stage audience. He can't, except in very unusual circumstances, give you feedback *during* the take. But his notes between them are the nearest equivalent so accommodate them as well as you can.

It can occasionally be tempting to think you know better than the director. Especially if he is inexperienced or preoccupied with the technical side of filming. I'm not going to pretend that all directors are wise. Some are simply journeymen, with a talent for organization and managing the process of production. But the good ones are sensitive and insightful. And all of them are seeing what the audience will see and giving you feedback on that. As you gain more experience, hopefully you will develop a deeper understanding of the relationship between what you do and how it comes across on screen. But, until then, trying to monitor your own performance from outside will pull you away from your real job: inhabiting the character's reality.

Concentration

The audience's demands on actors, whatever the medium, are completely unreasonable and contradictory. We want spontaneity as they deliver scripted and rehearsed lines. And we want them to be wholly truthful in completely artificial conditions, be it at 7.30 every night on a lit stage or recorded, fragment by fragment with all the contrivances of filming.

To create and sustain the imaginary circumstances all actors need a powerful ability to concentrate. But the radically different working conditions of stage and screen means the nature of the concentration differs considerably.

During the *'two hours traffic'* of a stage performance, the fictional reality is uninterrupted, apart from scene changes and an interval. Individual scenes tend to last for several minutes at least, sometimes much longer.

The rhythm of shooting is quite different. Most scenes on screen are much, much shorter than on stage – just 45–60 seconds – so the fictional world is created, repeatedly, for very short periods of time and you have to be 100 per cent committed to it at the start of every take. Almost every time the director calls *'cut'*, this is disrupted as people move in to adjust lamps, props, cables, etc. The director may come in and talk to you in that half-fiction, half-reality where you are both character and performer, usually addressing you by your real name but talking about *'you'* as the character. Then, with just a few seconds' notice, there's another take.

What's more, 11 hours is a long working day and this stop/start pattern can be extremely draining. It's like the difference between running 10,000 metres once and running 100 metres a hundred times.

Managing your energy

To do your best work in these very short bursts, you need to become an expert at turning on and off your concentration. And to do this you must take very seriously the task of managing your energy. Finding your own way to relax between takes and then crank up your concentration as the next take approaches is critical.

> John Hurt: *'When you're feeling inspired, concentration is the easiest thing in the world. But when it's not there you need to find a way to relax, to breathe deeply, to will yourself into the right mood. You have to know how to switch it on and off.'*

For most actors effective relaxation does not mean bantering with the other actors and generally being the life and soul of the shoot. Switching from amiably entertaining your colleagues with your favourite anecdote into the most intense concentration to inhabit fully another human being's emotional and physical reality does not happen so readily. Especially if, as happens so often in most actors' lives, you spent the previous days or weeks doing something other than acting so are a bit out of practice.

Yet it can be quite hard to maintain your focus. Many of the best actors I've worked with sit quietly between takes, often with their eyes closed, in 'neutral'. This can feel very alien to gregarious, vivacious, people-pleasing actors. In the hiatus between takes and set-ups, it may seem the most natural thing in the world to be friendly and pass the time of day with those around you. But the slightest, most fleeting lapse in concentration is immediately obvious on screen.

For some, 'relaxation' may mean something focused but emotionally undemanding – Sudoku, for example. Dustin Hoffman skips with a rope between takes. He talks about having bet the crew on *Tootsie* that he could skip for 45 minutes. And winning.

> Juliet Stevenson: *'The challenge is how to ignore the 35 people standing around. I try and stay in the bubble and not get pulled into chatting. I try to forget about the scene but stay in character.'*

Control your own mood

We are all influenced by the mood of those around us. This is often especially true of actors, many of whom are very sensitive to the emotional temperature. This sensitivity is precisely what will enable you to listen and respond to the performance opposite you.

But the mood of a group of 30 to 40 people working together, often under stressful and difficult conditions, can be very unpredictable. At times there may be a terrific sense of harmony and shared purpose. At others the atmosphere may be fractious and hostile with simmering tensions and periodic explosions. Most of the time this mood will be totally unrelated to your character's situation. So you need to be a master of generating your own mood. Doing so is another test of your powers of concentration.

Sound

This is an under-appreciated, but vital, part of filming. It's very easy for actors not to realize they have made a noise across their own, or others', dialogue by putting down a prop, scuffing their feet or similar. So you may find the boom operator asking you to remove your shoes or mime some action to prevent this. It can be disconcerting to be given another technical task to manage but it is essential: the sounds are needed, just not across dialogue. With experience you will learn to do this without being asked – it's all part of your awareness.

Wildtracks

Very often, at the end of a scene, there will be wildtracks. This means recording sound alone with the boom operator given free rein to put the microphone wherever he needs to. Sometimes this means dialogue, sometimes the footsteps and sometimes foley – other sounds that occur during the scene: clothes rustling, props being handled and so on. So you may, for example, be asked to walk through the scene, perhaps speaking the lines, perhaps not, but making all the natural accompanying noises.

30
ADDITIONAL DIALOGUE RECORDING (ADR)

You may be called upon to re-record lines of dialogue in a recording studio weeks or months after the shoot has finished. Recreating your emotional state is key to doing this well.

ADR

A regular feature of post-production is the need to re-record lines (and occasionally whole scenes) of dialogue because there was a problem with the synch sound recorded on the day – usually noises-off like traffic, background coughing or occasionally because it was off-mic. None of these are your fault. And sometimes new lines have been written to be delivered off-camera to clarify something.

It's likely to take place weeks after you shot the scene and you'll get paid a fee for doing it. You'll be called to a recording studio where the director will be supervising the whole thing. You stand in a soundproof booth, wearing headphones, and watch footage of the edited scene with whatever imperfections it contains.

There are then two types of ADR:

1 synching your voice to your in-vision lip movement
2 recording off-camera lines where there's no synch required.

The first is much harder because you have the added challenge of synching it to the pictures.

There are various ways this is done. Sometimes you'll be shown the footage and hear three 'pips' in your ears leading up to your line which begins where the fourth pip would have come. Sometimes you have the words as subtitles on the monitor with a mark bouncing along over the lines, like a karaoke, and you simply speak the line when it comes. Different methods suit different people. Personally, I found it easiest to ignore the footage entirely and listen carefully to the original recording and simply repeat that like a piece of music though, for some reason, recording engineers were often reluctant to allow me to do this.

The sound editor will lay the new recording over the pictures, and can even stretch some vowels a little, but the more closely you can mimic the original in terms of rhythm, breathing, pace, pitch, intonation, etc. the more likely it is to synch. The human ear is fantastically perceptive when it comes to sound, much more than we realize, and poorly done ADR really sticks out.

The hardest thing is to put yourself into the same emotional state as when you played the scene on the shoot, standing in a booth with headphones on, and in this it's much like working on radio. Weeks or months after you've moved on from the character and, with luck, are on another job can make it particularly hard.

ADR is likely to be your last involvement with any project before it's completed. Some actors find it enormously difficult, while some love it and regard it as an opportunity to improve on their original performance.

31
THE FINISHED PRODUCT

> There can be a sense of anticlimax about the screening of your work
> on TV. But it will be seen by more people than will ever see you on
> stage and it will exist forever.

Screening or broadcast

If it's a film or high-profile television production, there will be a premiere or press screening to which you'll probably be invited. But with some television, there's no screening, no applause and no real sense of achievement; just a feeling of anticlimax when it goes out. Getting the job is exciting. You do your preparation and put your heart into the shoot. Then, months later, it's on the telly one day. And that's it.

You may get a hard copy of the finished product from the production company through the post, but sometimes not. If there are reviews, they're unlikely to mention you unless you're playing a major part. No one recognizes you in the street. Hopefully your friends and family will watch and praise you. Some will forget, just as you'll sometimes forget to watch something a friend is in. But you'll be hurt because this is *your* work.

You might be surprised by what the director has decided to do with your performance. You may find your scenes have been trimmed or even cut entirely. With luck you'll be pleased, but sometimes you won't be.

Despite all this, I still believe it's the most fantastic medium for an actor and working on camera can be exhilarating. Unless it's a really obscure piece on a tiny TV channel, your work is seen by hundreds of thousands of people, far more than will ever see you on stage. And it exists forever: you can show your work to your grandchildren!

What's more it offers you the potential to work at a level of depth and detail that's unlike anything most theatre can aspire to, precisely because the camera comes so close. I'm not saying it's a better medium than the theatre but the emotional rewards of doing good work, work you're proud of, are enormously satisfying.

And it will make you a better stage actor. Drama schools throughout the Western world are still basically stage schools and it's my belief that they should put students on screen from the very beginning, rather than introducing *'acting for camera'* later like some peripheral supplement to the real art form of theatre. The camera's relentless scrutiny obliges actors to eliminate the performance gimmicks and come back to its core: living truthfully in imaginary circumstances.

32
PROFESSIONALISM

The film and television industry is not a place for amateurs. To have a career, you need to treat it as such, cultivate a deep professionalism and continue to develop your skills.

Punctuality

Be on time. It can be tempting to think that because you are creative you are not governed by the same rules as non-actors, including the need to be punctual. But film and television production is a business; time is money and you damage your employment prospects by being late. Your job is to be brilliant when the director calls 'action' and managing your time is a significant part of that.

This is not simply me being overly fussy about timekeeping. I am a late-aholic. I spent the first 10 years of my career routinely being late for castings and for jobs and, consequently, routinely underperformed and so persuaded people that they should not hire me in future. I am partially in recovery, but to this day I struggle with punctuality. I have learnt to recognize that being late is partly a way of managing my nerves. But it's not an intelligent or productive way of doing so. Now, when it matters, I get there on time.

Continue to train

One of the struggles for an actor is to keep in peak condition so that when work comes you are able to deliver at your very best.

Musicians know that if they don't practise for one day, they notice; if they don't practise for 2 days, the other musicians notice; if they don't practise for three days, the audience notices.

Athletes train every day. We would laugh at a sprinter who thought he could just turn up and run at his best without having trained in the months since his last race. But sadly this is exactly how many actors behave, apparently believing they can go to castings or a shoot, having spent the last few months working in a bar, and not doing any acting.

Now it's obvious how a musician or a dancer can practise. There are scales and exercises and stretches to do, classes to attend. But how does an actor practise?

First, there are the vocal and physical exercises that drama school will have given you. Admittedly it can be hard for an out-of-work actor to find the belief and motivation to practise. But this ongoing training does not have to be done alone. The Actors' Centre in London runs many types of class to help actors develop their skills. Acting classes in other cities come and go but there may be something nearer to you.

Sad to say, American actors are much more professional than British actors in this respect. In the United States it's intrinsically understood that part of the life of being an actor out of work is that you go to class. Doing classes are about much, much more than simply keeping yourself in trim. None of us leaves drama school complete, with nothing more to learn. Certainly, the Actors' Centre is a great place to learn more about acting on screen specifically and to practise it. And there are other places if you look.

Read plays and screenplays. Develop your understanding of good writing. There is a wealth of screenplays available to download free online. Discover the difference between writing for the screen and the stage. Read the scripts of films you have not seen. Read the lines out loud and find the rhythm of the scene. Practise your ability to do what they call in Hollywood 'hitting the notes'. Then watch the film and see how the experts do it.

Above all, keep your instrument tuned. By which I mean your body, your voice and your acting brain. It's a bitterly hard and frequently unfair profession. But while hard work is no guarantee of success, without it success is very unlikely to come your way.

ABOUT THE AUTHOR

Bill Britten studied psychology at Oxford University, then trained as an actor at the Central School of Speech and Drama in London. He worked as an actor in theatre and television before moving on to direct many films and episodes of television drama. As a director, his work has been BAFTA nominated and selected for the Cannes film festival.

He is a senior lecturer in Screen Acting and Directing at the Drama Centre at Central St Martin's, regularly runs workshops at the Actors' Centre and works internationally as a leadership and communications coach.

He lives in London with his wife and two children.

INDEX